VITALITY     IDEALISM     INDUSTRY

## Gaea

Gaea (jē'ȧ), was conceived by the Greeks as the lovely goddess Mother Earth. They represented her as the giver of life to all plants and animals.

In this picture she is lifting her bird and animal children to the sun so he may shine upon them and keep them warm. Her cupped hands signify her loving care and protection of all life on this earth. The poppies in her hair signify agriculture; for from Gaea spring the flowers, trees and the fruits. The grapes symbolize food. The fish in her hair and the seashells on her forehead remind us she is the mother of water life as well as of land life.

The word "Gaea," like the common words "geography" and "geology," is derived from the basic Greek word signifying "earth."

Volume Two contains the fascinating Story of Life. It is as beautifully written as a continued fairy tale— taking us step by step from the lowest to the highest forms of water, land and air life. Volume Two is dedicated to all forms of life, including fish, birds, trees, flowers and animals.

# OPTIMISM

By Dr. Frank Crane

ABOUT the most winning things in any boy or girl is the spirit of optimism.

That means, looking on the bright side of things.

There are always two sides to everything, and whether we see the dark or the light is very largely a matter of habit.

We all want to be liked, we want to be welcome, we want to be appreciated. And there is nothing in this whole world that is more likable and welcome and appreciated than cheer.

If you do not feel very well, conceal it as much as possible. That is not hypocrisy, it is simply consideration for other people's feelings.

If you are afraid, keep your fears to yourself. If you are in sorrow and trouble, do not talk about it.

Remember that other people have their own fears, troubles and sorrows, and it is a burden to them to have to bear yours also.

Nobody wants gloom. Everybody wants brightness.

If you are a girl, you naturally want to be loved, and a good thing for you to know is that it is not always the beautiful girls that are the best loved. It is the happy girls, those whose spirits are bright, whose words are cheery and whose enthusiasm is always present.

Nobody can help liking such persons.

Optimism is a word that comes from a Latin word meaning "the best." It implies thinking the best, looking for the best, and believing in the best.

And why not? None of us knows what is going to happen. Good luck may come, or bad luck. Tomorrow may be a happy day, or some trouble may appear. And as long as no one knows, why not believe that the best will come?

If you do believe this, it will make you strong and courageous and better prepared to meet whatever fortune the morrow may bring. While if you believe in some gloomy outcome, it will make you weak and nervous and unprepared.

We must remember that optimism is not a question that can be argued by facts. That is, no one can prove that things are going to turn out well, nor that they are going to turn out badly. Optimism is merely a state of mind. It is a point of view. It is a temper of the spirit.

And if we take this constant attitude of hope, and bright courage, it is going to make the world a better place to live in, and it is going to make us a better kind of people to live in it.

Optimism is a duty. The Bible says, "Rejoice, and again I say unto you, rejoice."

It is not only a duty, it is a privilege and an advantage. It makes life easier for us, and in every way we are better qualified to get along with people and succeed in our business than those whose outlook is always gloomy.

This

HOW and WHY PROGRAM of

CHILD MENTAL DEVELOPMENT

is registered

in the name of

THE COLEMAN CHILDREN

To whom

It was presented

For their information and education

By their Mommy and Daddy

# THE
# HOW AND WHY
# PROGRAM

## Little Questions That Lead
## to Great Discoveries

*By*

### MRS. ELEANOR ATKINSON

Author "Greyfriar's Bobby," "The Boyhood of Lincoln,"
"Johnny Appleseed," Etc.

*Advisory Editor*
LYON N. RICHARDSON, Ph. D.
Editor, Author, Dean, Director of Libraries

*Artists*

FREDERIC SWENEY
MARY HILKERT
JOHN CSOSZ
CARL HURLBUT

BETTY W. CLARK
JOHN CLAGUE
HOWARD BUTLER
HARLAN FARNUM

### KODACHROME BIRD PICTURES
By MAJOR ALLAN BROOKS, ARTIST, ORNITHOLOGIST

Used by Permission of The Audubon Society
American Nature Association, from Paintings by
R. BRUCE HORSFALL AND LYNN BOGUE HUNT

*Special History Stories*
RAYMON PEYTON COFFMAN

*Cover Designs*
GERALDINE VIRGINIA DEARBORN

PUBLISHED BY
THE L. J. BULLARD CO.
CLEVELAND, OHIO

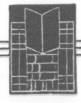

# TABLE OF CONTENTS
# THE HOW AND WHY PROGRAM
## NATURE UNIT

Page

Front Cover Story ............................................................................ 247
Optimism, by Dr. Frank Crane ....................................................... 248

## DEPARTMENT OF NATURE STUDY

"Nature Study," in the modern school, emphasizes first of all the things which the child can investigate most readily—flowers, trees, insects, birds, and animals. The following stories take him through the entire year and deal with the most important features of familiar plants, trees, insects and all the common varieties of birds and animals. The child's interest in nature is spontaneous, and through no other medium can his observation and reasoning powers be so easily developed ............................................................................ 254

### HOME GARDENS

Food Values of Vegetables ........................................................... 256
Vegetables That Make Us Grow ................................................... 258
How the Orchard Grew .................................................................. 262
Up Come the Sweetest Flowers .................................................... 265

### WILD FLOWERS

A Wild Garden and Its Tenants .................................................... 271
Little Lion Tooth and Its Cousin: Dandelion ............................... 275
A "Good Luck" Family: Clover ..................................................... 278
The Bonny Briar Bush: The Wild Rose Family .......................... 282

# TABLE OF CONTENTS

## THE HOW AND WHY PROGRAM (Continued)
## NATURE UNIT

### FOREST TREES

A Year in the Forest................................................ 286
Spring: "Rockaby Babies"........................................... 290
Summer: "In the Tree Tops"......................................... 297
Autumn: "When the Wind Blows"...................................... 301
Winter: "The Cradles Will Rock".................................... 305

### INSECTS

Mrs. Musca Domestica Calls: The Fly Tells Its Story................ 311
Mrs. Garden Spider "At Home"....................................... 317
Gulliver Man and His Lilliputian Enemies........................... 321
Pygmy Friends That Fly, Hop, and Creep............................. 325
Bees: Story of Bees, Wax, and Honey................................ 331

### BIRDS

Bird Songs and Colors.............................................. 342
Bird Nests and Babies ............................................. 350
Little Friends in Feathers......................................... 362

### WILD ANIMALS YOU WOULD LIKE TO KNOW

Big Brother Bear .................................................. 372
Pet Pussy and King Lion............................................ 378
"Here Come the Elephants".......................................... 385
The Animal Acrobat and Clown: The Monkey.......................... 395
The Ship of the Desert: The Camel................................. 404
Kangaroo and Opossum .............................................. 412
The Graceful Giraffe .............................................. 418
Mr. Nose Horn and Mr. River Horse: Rhinoceros and Hippopotamus... 422

### WILD AND DOMESTIC ANIMALS NEAR HOME

Mule Colt; Shetland Colt .......................................... 403
A long tramp over the country after a light snow fall and the footprints
    we found: Trails of tiny tracks in the snow.................427–437
Dogs .............................................................438–443

## ART THROUGH THE AGES

Art Through the Ages............................................... 444
Earliest Forms of Art.............................................. 445
Ancient Egyptian Art.............................. 446
Beauty of Grecian Art............................. 447
Great Works of Roman Art.......................... 449
Ornate Byzantine Art.............................. 451
Colorful Art of Persia............................ 452
Oriental Art of China............................. 453
Art in the Middle Ages............................ 454
The Magnificent Renaissance....................... 457
Baroque Art: 17th Century......................... 460
New Forms: 18th Century........................... 462
Paris and the 19th Century........................ 464
Art of Our Own Times............................. 468

# ILLUSTRATIONS
## NATURE UNIT

Home Vegetable Garden (color)................. 255
Peas, Squash, Eggplant, Pepper, Tomato, Pumpkin
    (color) .................................... 257
Broccoli, Radishes, Cauliflower, Lima Bean, Corn,
    Watermelon (color) ....................... 259
Carrot, Beans, Lettuce, Potato, Beet, Cucumber
    (color) .................................... 261
Red Raspberries, Blackberries, Apple, Peach,
    Strawberries, Pear, Plums, Cherries, Grape
    (color) .................................... 263
"And the Lord God planted a garden eastward in
    Eden" (color) ............................. 264
Rose, Chrysanthemum, Gladiolus, Portulaca, Morn-..
    ing-glory, Pansies (color)................. 266
Snapdragons, Calendula, Bachelor-buttons, Bleed-
    ing Heart, Dahlia (color)................. 268
Hepatica, Trillium, Jack-in-the-pulpit, Wild Aster,
    Meadow Lily (color) ...................... 270
Dandelion, Showing Plant, Flower and Seed Head (color)................. 272
Maple Flowers and Fruit; Pussy Willow Flowers................ 287
Birch Flowers and Fruit................ 288
Apple Blossoms and Roses (color)................ 289
Flowers—Chestnut, Honey Locust, Dogwood; Elm Fruit................ 295
Oak Flowers and Fruit................ 296
Trees—Bark, Leaf and Fruit: White Oak, Chestnut, Sycamore, Shellbark Hickory,
    Red Cedar, American Elm................ 306
Tree—Bark, Leaf and Bloom: Holly................ 307
Trees—Bark, Leaf and Fruit: Black Walnut, Sugar Maple................ 307
Trees—Bark, Needles and Fruit: Shortleaf Pine, Balsam Fir, White Spruce....... 307
Housefly (magnified)................ 311
Tsetse Fly (magnified)................ 312
Ichneumon Fly................ 312
A Fly's Foot Magnified................ 313
Protective Mimicry Among Insects (color)................ 315
Life Story of White Grub................ 316
A Spider and Its Web (color)................ 318
Hessian Fly (magnified)................ 322
Cotton Boll Weevil (magnified)................ 323
Dragonfly (color)................ 326
Ladybird (color)................ 327
Toad (color) ................ 328
Grasshopper ................ 329
Japanese Beetle ................ 329
Spraying from an Airplane to Kill Mosquitoes................ 330
Clothes Moth (magnified) ................ 330
Bee Life—Inside a Bee Hive................ 333
Bees—Worker, Queen, Drone, Pollen Basket................ 334
American, or Bald, Eagle (color)................ 335
Blue Grouse and Ruffed Grouse (color)................ 336
Common Birds in Their Natural Colors................338–339–340–341
Robin (color) ................ 343
Mockingbird (color) ................ 344
Brown Thrasher (color) ................ 345
Golden Plover (color)................ 346
Tree Swallow (color)................ 347
Crow (color) ................ 348
Birds' Nests and Eggs in Trees................ 351
Some More Birds' Nests and Eggs................ 352
Baltimore Orioles and Nest (color)................ 353
Egrets Nesting Forty Feet High................ 354
A Young Pelican's First Attempts at Fishing................ 354
Great Horned Owl ................ 357
Snowy Owl................ 357
Valley Quail and Mountain Quail (color)................ 358

# ILLUSTRATIONS (Continued)

Yellow-billed Cuckoo (color) ........ 360
Nesting Places for Birds ........... 361
Chestnut-backed Chickadee (color) .. 363
Vermilion Flycatcher (color) ........ 364
Sparrow Hawk (color) ............. 365
Mourning Dove (color) ............. 366
Mallards (color) ................... 368
Bird Flyways ...................... 369
Bird Tools ........................ 370
Bears ............................ 371
Cats ............................. 381
Lions, Tiger, Leopard .............. 382
North American Animals (color) .... 386
South American Animals (color) .... 387
African and Indian Elephants ....... 389
Elephants at Work ................. 390
Group of African Elephants ........ 394
Some Apes and Monkeys ........... 398
Four Kinds of Monkeys ............ 399

Mule Colt; Shetland Pony Colt ...... 403
Camels ........................... 405
Opossum (color) ................... 410
Spider Repairing Web (color) ....... 411
Beaver (color) .................... 411
Australian Animals (color) ......... 414
African Animals (color) ............ 415
Kangaroo and Nursery Pouch ....... 417
Giraffe ........................... 421
Rhinoceros ....................... 426
Hippopotamus ..................... 426
Rabbits .......................... 428
Animals Near Home in Woods, Fields
    and Rivers ................... 429
Porcupine (color) ................. 430
Otter with Fish (color) ............ 430
Wild Animals Near Home (color) . 433–434
Hunting With a Camera ........... 437
Dogs ........................... 438–443

## ART THROUGH THE AGES

Earliest Forms of Art (color) ....... 445
Early Art Objects .................. 445
Ancient Egyptian Art (color) ....... 446
From Temple at Luxor ............. 446
Egyptian Tomb Wall Painting ....... 446
The Sphinx, Cairo ................. 446
Beauty of Grecian Art (color) ....... 447
The Discus Thrower ............... 447
Porch of the Maidens, Athens ....... 447
Model of Parthenon, Athens ........ 448
Bronze Statuette: Horse ............ 448
Venus de Milo .................... 448
Great Works of Roman Art (color) .. 449
Bronze Statue: A Youth ............ 449
The Colosseum .................... 449
Model of Pantheon, Rome .......... 450
Trajan's Column .................. 450
Relief Carving, Sarcophagus ........ 450
Arch of Constantine ............... 450
Ornate Byzantine Art (color) ....... 451
Mosaic, Empress Theodora ......... 451
St. Mark's Cathedral, Venice ....... 451
Colorful Art of Persia (color) ....... 452
Persian Animal Rug ................ 452
Oriental Art of China (color) ....... 453
Porcelain Vase .................... 453
Bird on Flowering Branch .......... 453
Porcelain Water Pot ............... 453
Art in the Middle Ages (color) ..... 454
Notre Dame Cathedral, Paris ....... 454
Facade, Notre Dame, Paris ......... 454
Entrance, Cathedral, Strasbourg ..... 454
Part of Bayeux Tapestry ........... 455
Window, Exeter Cathedral .......... 455
Nave of Cathedral, Chester, England. 455
The Doge's Palace, Venice ......... 456
Cathedral Sculptures, Chartres ...... 456
The Magnificent Renaissance (color). 457
Baptistry Door .................... 457
St. Francis Preaching to the Birds ... 457
The Last Supper ................... 458
The Sistine Madonna .............. 458

St. Peter's Church, Rome ........... 458
Miracle of Loaves and Fishes ....... 459
The Cardinal ...................... 459
Saltcellar ......................... 459
Creation of Man ................... 459
Baroque Art: 17th Century (color).. 460
Children of Charles I .............. 460
Rembrandt's Son .................. 460
Palace of Versailles, Paris .......... 461
Girl with Jug ..................... 461
Portrait of a Lady ................. 461
New Forms: 18th Century (color) ... 462
Blue Boy ......................... 462
Monticello, Jefferson's Home ....... 462
Beckingham-Cox Wedding .......... 462
Don Manuel ...................... 463
Infanta Maria ..................... 463
Girl ............................. 463
George Washington ................ 463
St. Paul's Cathedral, London ....... 463
Paris and the 19th Century (color).. 464
Farm and Church .................. 464
Surrender of Lord Cornwallis ....... 464
Grand Canal, Venice ............... 465
Girl Making Garland ............... 465
Houses of Parliament, London ...... 465
Still Life ......................... 466
At Milliner's ...................... 466
The Gulf Stream ................... 466
Dancers Practicing ................ 467
By the Seashore ................... 467
Tahiti ............................ 467
Madame Ginoux ................... 467
Art of Our Own Times (color) ...... 468
July Hay .......................... 468
Residence—"Falling Water" ........ 468
S. C. Johnson Company Building .... 469
Red Studio ....................... 469
Three Musicians ................... 469
Menemsha Bight ................... 470
Midnight Ride of Paul Revere ...... 470
Madonna of the Trail .............. 470

# Foreword

## Nature Study

One day, in the middle of the nineteenth century, a group of young men in Harvard University was assigned a lesson in zoology by a new professor from Switzerland. He told them to study a live fish swimming in a tank. Every day for two weeks, the class was sent back to look again at that fish. Then the teacher went to the tank with his pupils, and gave a lecture an hour long on the things they had failed to see. The professor was Louis Agassiz. His method of teaching from the natural object gave such amazing results that he won worldwide fame. His classroom was crowded with eager students who afterwards, having learned to see what they looked at, made discoveries in the natural sciences.

It took a long time for Agassiz's nature study idea to work down into the pre-school life of the child. We get our knowledge of everything about us through our five senses—seeing, hearing, smelling, tasting, and feeling. The best time to begin to use these senses well is in the early years when young children eagerly reach for and try to handle everything they see. In the house, in the yard and garden just outside the house, parents have the opportunity to begin to lead even their tiny youngsters to a knowledge of the world about them. It is the parent's privilege to introduce to the child the world of living things,—flowers, vegetables, birds, insects, animals and trees. Any flower, tree, insect, bird or animal, truly seen, is just as inexhaustible as Agassiz's fish. The pre-school child may learn many things by helping care for these, and by watching them grow. One of the chief objects of nature study is the training of the power of observation. The successful person is the one who sees the most and best, and who understands the meaning and relation of things, and applies his knowledge.

The parent has the opportunity to lead his child to knowledge by encouraging the child's natural interest in living things. The stories in this book will help do this. A five-and ten-cent store magnifying glass, a microscope, a camera, and a specimen case are valuable helps to use, as the child grows older.

The Publishers.

*Who loves a garden still his Eden keeps,*
*Perennial pleasures plants, and wholesome*
*harvest reaps.*—AMOS BRONSON ALCOTT.

# FOOD VALUES OF VEGETABLES

| Vegetables | VITAMINS | | | | Proteins % | Carbohydrate % |
|---|---|---|---|---|---|---|
| | A | B₁ | B₂ | C | | |
| Asparagus | Good | Good | Good | Good | 2.2 | 3.9 |
| Beans (navy dry) | .... | Excel. | Excel. | .... | } 7.5 | 23.5 |
| Beans (snap) | Good | Good | Good | Good | | |
| Beans (lima, fresh) | Good | Excel. | Excel. | Good | | |
| Beets | .... | Good | .... | .... | 1.6 | 9.6 |
| Broccoli | Excel. | Good | Good | Excel. | 3.3 | 5.5 |
| Brussel Sprouts | .... | Good | Good | Good | 4.4 | 8.9 |
| Cabbage | .... | Good | .... | .... | 1.4 | 5.3 |
| Carrots | Excel. | Good | .... | .... | 1.2 | 9.3 |
| Cauliflower | .... | Good | Good | Excel. | 2.4 | 4.9 |
| Chard | Excel. | .... | Good | Good | 1.0 | 2.9 |
| Collards | Excel. | Good | Good | Good | 3.9 | 7.2 |
| Corn (sweet, yellow) | Good | Good | Good | .... | } 3.7 | 20.5 |
| Corn (sweet, white) | .... | Good | .... | Good | | |
| Cress | Excel. | Good | Good | Good | 1.7 | 3.3 |
| Dandelions | Excel. | .... | Good | Good | 2.7 | 8.8 |
| Endive | Excel. | Good | Good | Good | 1.6 | 4.0 |
| Kale | Excel. | Good | Excel. | Excel. | 3.9 | 7.2 |
| Kohlrabi | .... | .... | .... | Excel. | 2.1 | 6.7 |
| Lettuce (head) | .... | Good | .... | .... | } 1.2 | 2.9 |
| Lettuce (green) | Excel. | Good | .... | Good | | |
| Muskmelons | .... | .... | .... | Good | 0.6 | 5.9 |
| Okra | .... | Good | .... | Good | 1.8 | 7.4 |
| Parsnips | .... | Good | .... | Good | 1.5 | 18.2 |
| Peas (dry) | .... | Excel. | Excel. | .... | } 6.7 | 17.7 |
| Peas (green) | Good | Excel. | Good | Good | | |
| Peppers | Excel. | .... | Good | Excel. | 1.4 | 6.2 |
| Potatoes (sweet) | Excel. | .... | Good | Good | 1.8 | 27.9 |
| Potatoes (white) | .... | Good | .... | Good | 2.0 | 19.1 |
| Pumpkins | Excel. | .... | .... | .... | 1.2 | 7.3 |
| Rhubarb | .... | .... | .... | Good | 0.1 | 3.8 |
| Spinach | Excel. | Good | Good | Excel. | 2.3 | 3.2 |
| Squash | Excel. | .... | .... | .... | 1.5 | 8.8 |
| Tomatoes | Good | Good | .... | Good | 1.0 | 0.4 |
| Turnips | .... | .... | .... | Good | 1.1 | 7.1 |
| Turnip Tops | Excel. | Good | Excel. | Good | | |

Peas

Squash

Eggplant

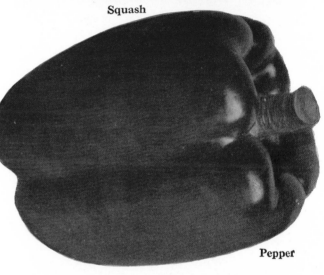

Pepper

Tomato

Pumpkin

# Vegetables That Make Us Grow

Early in the spring, when there was no danger of frost, the doctor spaded his garden. The vegetables he had planted last year had taken their food from the soil. They had eaten nitrogen, potash, phosphorus, and minerals. So the doctor put these elements back in the soil in the form of fertilizer.

A little boy and girl who lived next door came over to watch the doctor. "Isn't it wonderful," said the doctor, that plants can eat the elements in the earth. By the aid of sunlight and the green chlorophyll in the leaves, plants change the elements into starch, sugar, fat, and vitamins. So plants make the food which animals eat. Without plants, animals could not live."

The doctor then began planting the seeds, taking care to cover them to a depth of four times their thickness. Some of the smaller seeds he barely covered over. He made the rows run north and south, so the plants would get the most sunlight possible. He was careful to walk only between the rows, so as not to press the soil too hard over the seeds. Tomatoes and cabbage took a long time to grow, so he set out young plants which he had bought at the greenhouse.

"You children," said the doctor, "eat vegetables which once grew only in places far away. Beets and watermelons first grew in Africa. South America was the first home of eggplants, squash, peppers, and tomatoes. White potatoes came from Chili, Peru, and Mexico, and sweet corn from Peru. Pumpkins, sweet potatoes, and beans came from tropical America. Lettuce, radishes, onions, and rhubarb were first grown in Asia, and spinach and muskmelons in Persia. From Europe the white settlers of America brought asparagus, broccoli, parsnips, peas, and turnips.

"All vegetables really taste good," continued the doctor, "when you get used to them. It is fun to learn to like all vegetables, just as it is fun to play many different kinds of games."

The doctor did not plant his garden all at one time. Every ten days for a month he planted a few yards of corn, peas, beans, and lettuce, so they would ripen at different times and he would have fresh vegetables for his table for many weeks from his garden. When his lettuce and other early vegetables had been picked, he would plant turnips in their place.

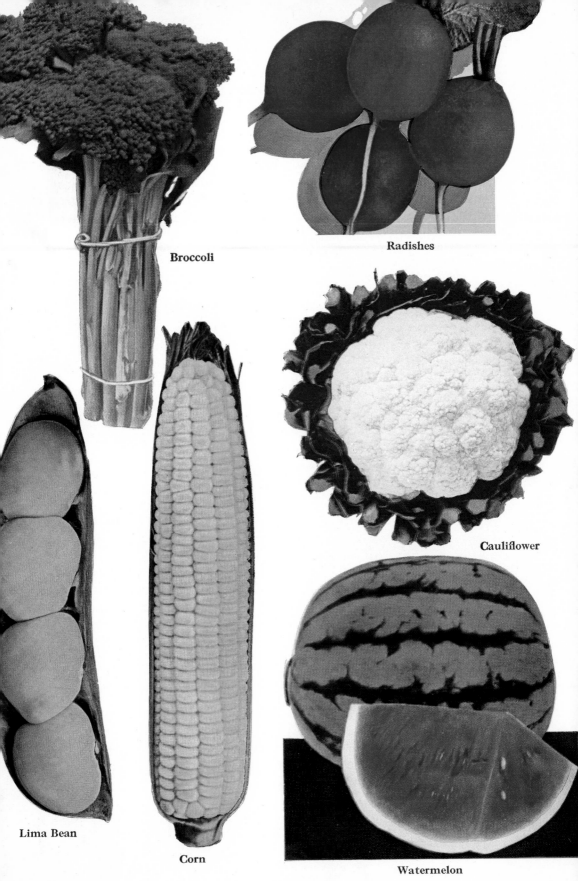

Broccoli

Radishes

Cauliflower

Lima Bean

Corn

Watermelon

In his office the doctor had a chart which told what kinds of food were in each vegetable. He showed the children the chart. It was like the one printed in this book. Carbohydrates, or starch and sugar, build our bodies and give us energy and warmth. The vegetables richest in starch are, in order, sweet potatoes, white potatoes, sweet corn, and peas. Those richest in sugar are parsnips, carrots, onions, rutabagas, watermelons, sweet potatoes, muskmelons, and sweet corn.

The proteins in vegetables and meats help build muscle, and the fats keep our bodies warm. The vegetables richest in proteins are beans, peas, brussel sprouts, collards, kale, sweet corn, and broccoli. The fats are found especially in sweet corn, dandelions, sweet potatoes, asparagus, collards, kale, parsnips, brussel sprouts, and peas. Then there are the vitamins. $A$ helps us to grow and is good for our eyesight. $B$ and $B_1$ are good for our nerves and keep us from being peevish and cross. $C$ gives us good bones and digestion. The vegetables richest in all four vitamins are, in order: kale, fresh lima beans, broccoli, spinach, turnip greens, collards, cress, endive, green peas, asparagus, and snap beans. These vegetables, too, are richest in the minerals which the body needs, especially in calcium and iron.

The doctor also planted some raspberry and blackberry bushes at the north end of his lot, and he grew some grapevines along a fence. There were two kinds of raspberries, the black ones and the red ones. The black ones had always grown in America. Some of our red raspberries came from Europe. The table grapes were black Concords, white Niagaras, and red Catawbas and Delawares. Each year long, new, green shoots would grow on the grapevines and berry bushes. No fruit grew on them the first year. But the next year these shoots became brown on the outside with a kind of bark, and the doctor called them canes. The canes bore fruit. When the fruit was all picked, the doctor would cut off the canes so that the roots could supply more food to the new, green shoots which would become canes next year and bear fruit. When the doctor wished to start new bushes or vines, he would bend a long, new shoot along the ground and cover it with soil at several places. At these places new shoots would sprout, and the doctor would have a new grapevine or raspberry or blackberry bush.

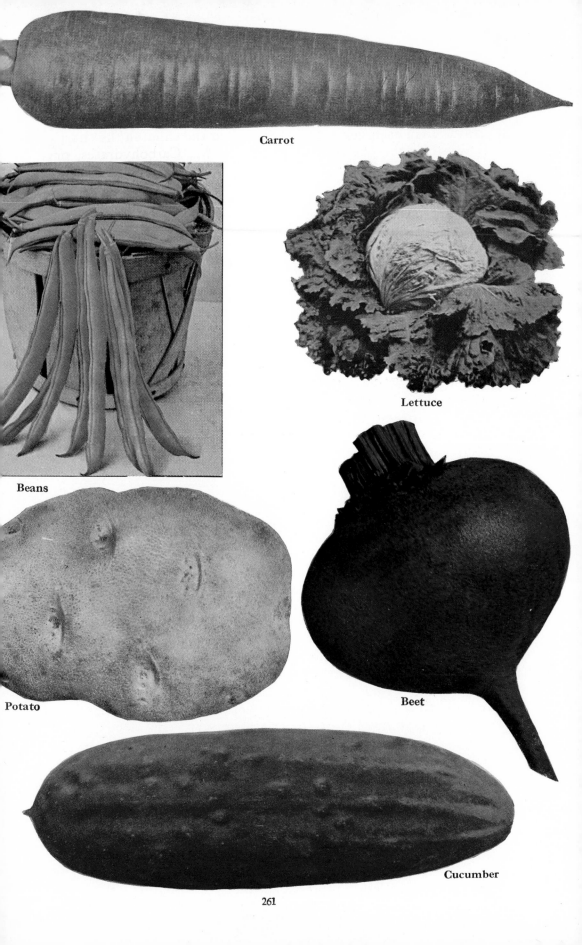

Carrot

Lettuce

Beans

Potato

Beet

Cucumber

# How the Orchard Grew

In the spring the children played on swings in the doctor's orchard. The pink and white blossoms made a great fragrant flower garden. Later the cherries began to ripen, and then the peaches, plums, pears, and apples as the summer days passed.

"Hundreds of years ago," said the doctor, "there were no apple trees. Men developed them from thorny wild rose brier bushes growing in Asia Minor. So the apple is a child of the rose." The doctor had Yellow Transparent and red Melba apples for summer, red McIntosh for autumn, and Jonathan, Red Spy, Baldwin, and Golden Delicious apples for winter.

"Peach trees probably first grew in Iran or Persia," said the doctor. "The Greeks gave them their name, which means 'Persian apple.' They are cousins of the rose and of the almond. Peach seeds still look much like almond nuts."

"Pears are also related to roses," the doctor told the children. "But unlike other fruits, you must pick pears before they are quite ripe, and allow them to ripen in a cool place. Pears become gritty if they ripen on trees.

"Plums and prunes are cousins of peaches," continued the doctor. "There are yellow, and red, and purple-black plums. The European and Asiatic varieties are the ones most commonly grown. You must plant several trees in the same orchard or they will not bear fruit. The pollen of one tree must be blown by the wind or carried by insects to the blossoms of another tree, or fruit will not grow. This is also true of most sweet cherry trees, the Bartlett pear tree, and the Baldwin and Rhode Island Greening apple trees."

The doctor told the children that cherry trees were developed in Europe and Asia. He had in his orchard sour Baldwin cherries for pies, and several sweet cherry trees, among them the Windsor red, the Bing dark red, and the Napoleon yellow.

"I bought these fruit trees at a nursery," the doctor said, "where the men had planted seeds. After the seeds grew to be baby trees the men cut twigs or buds from large fruit-bearing trees and grafted them on the baby trees to make them bear the best fruit."

Red Raspberries

Blackberries

Apple

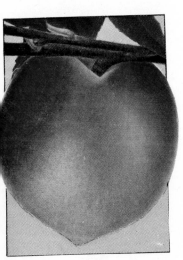

Peach

Strawberries

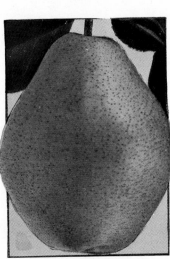

Pear

Plums

Cherries

Grape

263

*And the Lord God planted a garden eastward in Eden.*
—Genesis: II, 8.

# Up Come the Sweetest Flowers

The cold winter days were past. Spring had come. The sun was warm in the bright afternoons. Little Mary had seen the first robin of the season hopping on the ground looking for worms. Spring had unlocked the earliest flowers "to paint the laughing soil." Along the garden paths blooms had burst forth. The small white snowdrops and the white and yellow crocus buds had opened almost before the snow had melted. Last year, Mary's little brother George had brought blue violets and yellow adder's tongue plants from the woods, and had planted them at the side of the house which was shady much of the day. This spring both Mary and George had watched them grow.

Some days later larger flowers had blossomed. Mary and George went over to the doctor's yard to see the bed of goblet-shaped tulips, white and yellow and red ones, which the doctor's wife had planted several years before. The doctor's wife took the children along a garden walk. They could smell the sweet-scented pink and blue hyacinths, and the fragrant white and yellow narcissus blooms, and the yellow-belled daffodils, and the jonquils which the children thought smelled as sweet as the hyacinths.

A little later in the spring the children came again to the doctor's garden to see the white and blue iris, with large and lovely crinkled petals, growing in the rear of the lawn. The doctor's wife gave George a large pink peony and Mary a white one.

The thick, fleshy bulbous roots of the spring flowers had slept in the ground all winter, and had begun to grow when the sun first warmed the earth. The doctor's wife called the flowers perennials because the roots had not died in the wintertime, and flowers sprang up from them each year. Each year, too, new baby bulbs had grown around the older bulbs. The doctor's wife gave some of the new bulbs to Mary and George so that they could plant them and start flower gardens of their own.

New plants may be grown in several ways. The doctor's wife gave Mary and George some aster seeds to plant in a small bed. Then she showed them how some plants will grow new roots from their stems. She cut a slip from a geranium plant, with a leaf on

Rose

Chrysanthemum

Gladiolus

Portulaca

Morning-
Glory

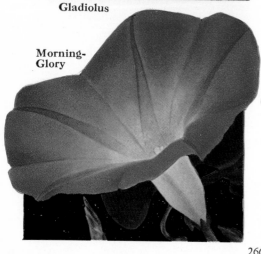

Pansies

it, and gave it to the children. They put it in a glass of water. After a number of days new roots grew from the bottom of the stem, and the children had a new geranium plant. They put it in rich earth in a flower pot. They also cut a begonia leaf across the larger veins and stuck the cut end of the leaf in sand and water. After a time new roots grew from the ends of the veins.

In the doctor's yard there were flowers blooming from early spring until late fall. After the early flowers had bloomed, other kinds blossomed in late spring and early summer. Yellow and blue larkspur spikes, pink and red poppies, pink and blue phlox, bachelor's buttons, and Canterbury bells filled the yard with colors. They waved and laughed in the bright summer sun. And then later in the summer and in the autumn came the spiked gladiolus flowers in many colors, and dahlias, mignonette, delphinium, cannas, late lilies, asters, tall hollyhocks, chrysanthemums in red and bronze, and yellow golden glow and sunflowers.

The children especially liked the roses. There were small bushes of tea roses, and larger bushes of old-fashioned roses which were most fragrant, and climbing rose vines, and two tree roses. Some of the roses bloomed first in the spring, and twice again during the summer months. There were many colors—white and ivory, and many shades of yellow, pink, red, orange, and russet. Unlike most flowers, roses grew best in well-drained clay soil.

Years ago the doctor's wife had planted formal flower beds. But in recent years she had arranged her flowers informally along the sides and rear of the lawn, and in certain places around the house and porch.

Mary and George noticed that she had planted the tallest flowers in the back rows, and the shorter flowers in front of them, and the shortest flowers in the very front rows. The tallest flowers were the hollyhocks, sunflowers, cosmos, cornflowers, cannas, delphinium, and gladioluses. In front of these flowers were the shorter stemmed asters, poppies, zinnias, petunias, carnations, calendula, and phlox. And in front of them came the pansies, forget-me-nots, verbenas, lilies-of-the-valley, sweet alyssum, and portulaca.

Most flowers grow best in sunny places where there is a bit of shade during a part of the day. But some kinds of flowers like lots of sun, and other kinds like lots of shade. In the sun-

Snapdragons

Calendula

Bachelor
Buttons

Bleeding-
Heart

Dahlia

268

niest places the doctor's wife planted tulips, sweet William, purple columbine, white and yellow daisies, dahlias, phlox, buttercups, sunflowers, asters, hollyhocks, golden glow, and cornflowers. In the shady places she planted lilies-of-the-valley, lady's slippers, red bleeding hearts, lilies, and primroses.

The children liked to sit on the great porch along the side of the house. It was a cool place to rest after they had been playing in the sun. Flowering vines grew up the sides of the porch, climbing all the way to the top. There was a sweet-scented white and yellow flowering honeysuckle vine that bloomed in the spring. And there was a Chinese wisteria loving the sun, and a large-petaled lavender-blue clematis vine that liked a bit of shade. A Virginia creeper bloomed in the summer, and some climbing roses came out in late spring and again in the summer. The porch was such a lovely place for quiet games!

Most flowers grow best in a rich loamy earth that is easily crumbled in the hands. This earth is rich in humus, which is decayed vegetation. Plants must eat even as children do. Manure, peat moss, and decayed leaves and grass are the best of natural foods for plants.

"Do you know," the doctor's wife asked Mary and George, "why I planted golden glow at the side of the garage? I'll tell you. Yellow is the brightest color, and I wished to make this spot very bright. The warmest colors are red, orange, and brown. The coolest colors are white, blue, and gray; the most restful colors are violet and green."

"I see now why you put the reclining chair on the porch beside the honeysuckle vine," said George. "The green leaves are restful, and the white flowers make one feel cool."

"Yes," said the doctor's wife. "When I wish brilliant effects, I plant flowers near together which have blossoms of complementary colors. Very beautiful combinations are made by placing orange-colored flowers and blue flowers close together, and yellow flowers near violet and purple flowers, and red flowers against a green background of thick leaves."

"Thanks for telling us so much about flowers and colors" said George. As the children were ready to go home, the doctor's wife gave them some pansy seeds to plant, because pansies are orange and blue and yellow and violet.

Hepatica

Great White Trillium

Jack-in-the-Pulpit

Wild Aster

Meadow Lily

# A Wild Garden and its Tenants

This is the story of a wild garden that was found near a public school on the edge of a big city. None of the children had the tiniest garden, and they were not allowed to pick flowers in the park, even to use in the school room for nature study. So this wild garden, where they could pick armsful of flowers, where they could pull plants up by the roots, where they could gather seed cases and cocoons, and watch insects at work, was a wonder and delight.

Even the teachers did not know it was a garden, at first. It was a vacant block of land two hundred feet square. All around it ran a new cement walk. The ground was two or three feet below the level of the street and would cost a good deal to fill in. Perhaps that was why there were no houses on it. The soil was very poor. From the walks the earth crumbled away in steep banks of gravel, sand and yellow clay. Water lay in sunken places, making frozen ponds for sliding in winter. There were a fallen tree-trunk and two or three rotting stumps of scrub oaks, around which mosses and low ferns grew. In the spring the ground was boggy, and scantily covered with ragged weeds and wire grass. Strips of blue grass turf below the walk, were dotted with the golden heads of the dandelion. In the wettest places a few clumps of blue flag lilies and pussy willows were found. Along one bank were brambles that, in June, blossomed the single pink flowers of the wild rose. And there were clover blossoms.

But that was all. When school closed in June the lot was covered with tall, coarse, ill-smelling weeds that gave no promise of flowers. But when school opened in September, the place was a jungle of purple and yellow, with swarms of winged visitors.

On the strip of green sod under the edge of the walks, the dandelions still showed bud and blossom and gauzy seed globe. But they did not take all the space. The grass was thick with the trefoil leaves and round buttons of white clover. And here and there was the glossy-leafed, pink-flowered spike of smart weed. Clambering up the bank grew a strong, rough-stemmed little vine with leaves

271

DANDELION, SHOWING PLANT, FLOWERS AND SEED HEADS

Dear common flower, that grow'st beside the way,
Fringing the dusty road with harmless gold.
—James Russell Lowell.

like a wild strawberry. At every twisted whorl of leaves was a tiny, star-like flower, as yellow as a butter-cup. It was the cinquefoil. Cinquefoil means five-leaved, as trefoil means three, so the little vine really was a far away cousin of the strawberry. Among the cinquefoil were clumps of mint. Their long, hairy stems and fuzzy leaves were topped with frowzy heads of lavender-pink, fringed with silver and breathing spicy smells. In every corner, and in many a crack of the sloping bank, stout burdocks were rooted. The pinkish-purple-topped green burs, in heavy knots, leaned out over the walk to catch in the clothing of passersby.

Farther afield tall thistles lifted royal purple heads, crowned with plush. They had a soldier guard of sharp lances and spears set on stem and leaf and flower. But, unafraid, wild morning glory vines twined around their spiny columns and hung out delicate pink and red and white flower bells. The morning glories clambered up the dusty stalks, and bloomed among the small, pale, yellow flowers of the mulleins.

In that wild garden were four varieties of clover—the white, creeping clover of blue-grass lawns; the pinkish purple-headed clover of farm meadows; the tall, shrub-like sweet clover, with tassel blossoms of white, and a blood-red clover, with pointed heads like pine cones. The crimson clover is a foreigner. Grown all over Europe, it is not often seen in America. In that wild garden it was a well-born emigrant among hardy and rough American weeds.

Except for the clovers, the smart weed, the morning glories, the white parasols of tansy, the mint and a few fiery spikes of the cardinal flower, the garden was a haze of yellow, spotted with purple. The long plumes of the golden-rod made a background for everything else. Against its feathery masses were set the dazzling yellow of the field sun flowers and black-eyed Susans. Much of the mustard had gone to seed. The tall plants were hung with tiny green pods, but there were still some clusters of yellow, cross-shaped flowers.

Lower down, hidden in wire grass, were yellow-flowered sorrel, with acid leaves that the children liked to nibble. There was many a sturdy bunch of butter and eggs, with their cream and gold, lipped and spurred blossoms set on spikes, the country cousin of the snap-dragons of gardens. There were seed spikes and broad leaves of dock and plantain; the peppery seed sprays of the tongue grass, that gave a feast to all the pet canaries in the neighborhood, and the catnip mint that made pet pussies go into spasms of delight. But these plants only added to the green of the leaves. The purple notes in the riot of yellow were given by the royal heads of the thistles, the reddish purple spikes of the iron weed, and the violet and lavender ray-flowered clusters of wild asters.

For several days the children were puzzled by an odor as sweet as that of lilies of the valley. It could be smelled only at night, when the garden lay dim and dewy under the moonlight. The perfume was traced to weedy stalks with small green-sheathed buds. They were not noticed by day, but opened pale, yellow, five-petaled rose-shaped flowers, after night fall. It was the evening primrose that grew in the shelter of dense thickets of golden-rod and asters. Big moths visited the primrose by night. In the day time the shriveled blooms held drops of honey so sweet that wasps with steel blue wings passed all the open flowers by, to drink that nectar.

Above the whole field insects were always on the wing. A little white butterfly was fond of the purple thistle. Bumble bees visited the thistles, the field clover and the butter-and-eggs. It was very funny to see a heavy, buzzing black and yellow bumblebee drop on the lower lip of a butter-and-eggs blossom, tip it down and force its greedy head into the long honey-filled spur. Little honeybees liked the white clover best. The goldenrod plumes, when in full blossom and gold-dusty with pollen, were always spotted with little black beetles that could scarcely be shaken off. This same little jetty beetle liked the dandelion pollen, too.

Gauze-winged dragon flies darted here and there; grasshoppers by hundreds leaped and clicked their wings, and robins and jay birds from a nearby park made raids on the grasshoppers. A dozen varieties of butterflies were seen by day, and many a moth by night. On every dewy morning the webs of spiders were strung with diamonds. The caterpillars had spun their cocoons on the stoutest of the weed-stalks, and flies grew sluggish in the cool nights. In dry places, and between the cracks of the walks, were little domes of sand, honey-combed with tiny holes. These were doors to underground houses of red and black ants.

Soon there were many seeds flying about—seeds of the dandelion, the thistle, the goldenrod, the milkweed. There were seeds with tails and wings and gauzy sails, and hooks and bursting pods. Every breeze loosened and scattered them. When frost came and killed the blossoms, the garden was a feeding ground for birds that ate the scarlet hips of the wild roses and the seeds of weeds.

# Little Lion Tooth and its Cousins

In the spring, the grass that bordered the cement walk around the wild garden was not two inches high before it began to be dotted with the golden rosettes of the dandelion. When the warm fingers of the children closed around a bunch of short stems, the flowers soon closed into green-sheathed buds that refused to open again. So a boy who didn't like to come to school, but who did like to roam in the fields and woods, was sent to bring in a whole plant. He was gone an hour, but he brought a fine plant, and such a fine story of how he got it that he fairly ran back to school.

At first he tried to pull a plant up by the root. But the flower stems and leaves broke away. Then he dug around the base of a plant a little way, and got hold of the crown of the root. That snapped an inch below the ground, breaking off a stout root half an inch thick. At last he went home and got a long, thin-bladed table knife, that he sank in the soil to the handle and slipped all the way around the root to loosen the soil. When he pulled, the root snapped six inches under ground, leaving the tip buried there. Then— for he was a clever, determined boy who wouldn't give up, something like a dandelion in that—he dug a trench around the plant and sank the knife deeper. He tried six times before he got a whole, unbroken root. But he got it!

"Bravo! Stout little lion-tooth; you know how to hold on!" said the teacher, clapping her hands. The children were puzzled. Did she mean the boy or the plant? Perhaps both.

"Lion-tooth?" cried a dozen excited voices. Why, yes. The French people long ago noticed that this wayside flower has a narrow, tooth-notched leaf, so they called it *dent-du-lion*. In England, where the meaning of the name was not known, it was changed to dandelion. You know a tooth doctor is a *dent*-ist. Very likely the lion part of the name was given because this kind of plant is king of all plants, as the lion is king of the animals. The English people had a name of their own for it. They called it Peasant's Clock. A peasant is a farmer. Farmers have to get up early and go to bed early. The dandelion opens its yellow eye at four o'clock and shuts it at eight or nine—a very good clock for farmers. Another old

English name for it is Blow Ball, because of its gauzy, feathered seed globe that every wind scatters.

The root of the dandelion is round, rough tapering from crown to tip, almost black on the outside, brittle but tough, hollow in the middle, giving it strength with lightness, and with many root-hair water suckers. The leaves grow in spreading, flattened circles from the crown, with the flower stems set around the inner circle. Rain, falling on leaves and flowers, drains right into the hollow root. So the dandelion begins to use water at once.

The dandelion opens day after day, the blossom head growing larger, and its stem stretching and lengthening into a hollow, rubbery pipe. When pulled the stem stretches a little, like rubber, before it snaps. And out of the broken end, oozes a thick milky sap that stains the hands brown and makes them feel sticky. The sap of the rubber tree is a thick, milky fluid much like that of the dandelion. The dandelion has some rubber, resin, sugar, and a bitter medicine in its sap. Do you know of any other milky-sapped plants? Milkweed!

Did you ever split a hollow stem of dandelion in strips, and pull it through your mouth to make a bunch of curls? It tasted bitter, didn't it? Every part of the plant has that bitter taste, very strong in the old roots, just a hint in the young leaves. In the country, people often gather the young leaves of dandelion with mustard and curly dock leaves, and cook them for greens. They are better than spinach. The French use their dent-du-lion leaves for salad, as we use lettuce. Indeed, lettuce is a cousin of the dandelion, so is chicory or endive, another salad plant.

When there were plenty of blossoms of the dandelion everywhere, each child brought a big one, as round and yellow and as many rayed as a baby sun, to school. They traced the circles of yellow strap-shaped petals, and tried to count the sunny rays. They got their finger tips all gold-dusty with pollen and learned, in that way, how the honey bees and butterflies carry pollen away on their legs. They found that the rays all had their stems sunk in a soft, green vase. With sharp finger nails they split the sides of the vases and spread them open. The rays just fell apart, so one could be picked out and studied under a microscope. Growing upward from the little swollen base of each ray, were shining threads tipped with buttons or pollen dust—seed makers!

"Why," said a surprised little girl, "just this yellow ray and the things growing on it look like a whole flower!"

"It is.  A dandelion head is a whole bouquet of flowers in a cup."

"It's something like a United States of flowers, isn't it?" asked a boy.

"That's it!  A great scientist has said that the motto of the dandelion and its cousins seems to be 'United we stand'."

Really, the dandelion might be chosen for our national flower. It grows everywhere; it blooms from April until frost, and it is hard to conquer, once it gets a foothold.  Its root goes deep and lives over winter.  You may cut the plant off, burn the ground over, or plow it up, but the smallest root tip sends up a new plant.  Every seed globe scatters it far.  Count the seeds of the Blow Ball.  Sturdy, determined little Lion Tooth, it hangs onto every one of its thousand chances of life.

There is another reason why it might be a good national flower.  Its ray flowers, its toothed leaves, its long, swaying stems and gauzy seed globes could be used in many beautiful forms of art.  They could be used as rosettes and borders, and the bases and capitals of stone pillars.  See what pretty designs in charcoal, crayon and water color you can make from studies of the dandelion.

These many-in-one flowers are called composites.  All the ray flowers belong to this family—the daisy, the sun-flower, the asters, the chrysanthemums, dog fennel, rosinweed, thistles, the —guess!  But you never will—the goldenrod!

The composite flowers are the highest in the plant world because they can live and grow, and make and scatter the most seed under the hardest conditions.  They are not at all concerned about being useful to men.  Nearly one-eighth of all the plants on the globe are composites, but many of them are troublesome weeds.  The daisy, the aster and the chrysanthemum have been improved into beautiful garden flowers, and the lettuce and endive into salad plants.

The whole insect world seems to help these composite flowers. Bees and wasps and flies and beetles visit them.  Moths suck their honey by night.  They have enemies, too.  Grasshoppers eat their leaves.  Crickets and beetles lay eggs on them.  Caterpillars bore tunnels down goldenrod stems.  The aphis, or plant louse, sucks their juices.  But the ant, the red spider, the insect-eating birds, and toads and frogs find a thicket of goldenrods and asters a fine hunting ground, and destroy these enemies.

# A "Good Luck" Family

Did you ever find a four-leafed clover? It's good luck to find one. With a four-leafed clover in your shoe you can walk right in among goblins and witches in any fairy story, and they can't play tricks on you. Long, long ago people thought any clover leaf was a charm. Most clover leaves have three leaflets, and three is a lucky number. Besides, many of the leaflets are marked with white, daintily penciled horseshoes, and everybody knows a horseshoe is lucky. But ask any farmer and he will tell you that clover is a good luck plant, whether it has three leaflets or four, or is marked with a horseshoe or not. When you read this story you will find out why.

Clover is one flower that you can always find in June, and June is the leafy month when there are few flowers. The spring blossoms are gone, the orchards are done blooming. But there are acres and acres of purple-pink clover heads in blossom, all over the land, and more acres of the violet-purple clusters of alfalfa, a first cousin of the clovers. The round buttons of the white, creeping clover dot every green lawn, and the blood red cones of the crimson clover grow along many a wayside.

How far one can smell a field of clover! It is a breath of the country as sweet as the perfume of orchards in bloom. Over a clover field there is always a pleasant hum of bumblebees and honey bees, and the glimmer of wings of gay little butterflies. When the feast of the clover is spread all the winged world goes to the party. Let us go, too.

Look out for Mr. Bumble Bee in a clover field! Big, fuzzy, black and yellow worker, he isn't thinking about you at all. But he blunders about, bumping into things, and he thinks human beings are enemies, as they very often are. He's a good friend of the red clover, and he often makes his nest in the ground near the roots. He drops on a fine flower head and pokes his long honey-sucker mouth to the bottom of the flower tubes. Pull one of those flowers yourself, and suck the base of it. You get a sweet drop, don't you? The white clover is sweet, too, but the honey bee feeds on that. The tubes of the white clover are short, and the bumble bee has a regular fishing pole of a mouth, too long for such shallow pools of nectar.

White clover is called the honey suckle of the grass, and bee keepers often plant whole fields of it.

Because it has so many flowers on one head, you may think the clover is a cousin of the dandelion. It isn't. The flowers are not crowded into a green vase, they just grow very close together on the swollen end of a stem. Pull the colored tubes from a clover head, and you will see that you have left behind every one some tiny upright threads. Those are the seed-making parts. Put a pink tube under a microscope and see how it widens, at the top, into pouting lips something like a sweet-pea blossom. Clover and alfalfa are really cousins of the peas and beans and peanuts, and other plants that ripen their seeds in pods. You know the pods of peas and beans that you can split to shell out the seeds? Clover seed, too, grow—one or two, in a fairy pod below the tubular blossom. It is hidden, for the flower tube dries and turns brown on the head. The pod of the peanut is a woody, papery shell that grows on buried stems like potatoes. The seed-pods of alfalfa are coiled in snail-like spirals, and the teeny weeny seeds of green or yellow are exactly the shape of kidney beans.

How much a sweet-pea blossom looks like a butterfly. One of the names of this class of plants is a long Latin word that means butterfly. You can always know them by the blossom, although some of them are low creepers and some are beautiful trees. Do you like licorice candy? Licorice is a cousin of the clover and peanut. It is a woody shrub sometimes called the sweet root, for it is from its root that the licorice juice is made. The sensitive plant, whose leaves go to sleep if you touch it, is one of this family, too; and the indigo shrub that gives us our beautiful blue dye. Another very tall relation is the beautiful honey locust tree, with its clusters of pink butterfly blossoms. It grows in many parts of our country. The clovers are members of a very big, important family, aren't they? They are all great honey makers.

All of these butterfly-blossomed, pod-seeded plants have strong, fibrous roots. There is a central root-stock with many branches, and a bush of rootlets, like a leafless shrub turned upside down and buried. This gives them a strong hold on the soil and many water suckers. Their stems are very zig-zaggy, branching in a twisty kind of way, as if they didn't quite know whether to be vines or not. The white clover, and the dear little shamrock of Ireland, spring from creeping, vine-like stems. Many peas and beans climb on poles, or on other plants like cornstalks. Alfalfa is more bushy, with smaller leaflets than the clovers. The acacia, the sensitive plant, and locust have long, feather-veined fern-like leaves.

Beside the bees, the pod-seeded plants have another animal friend. He lives in the ground, on the roots. He is so small you can not see him except with a very good microscope. But you can find the house he lives in with hundreds of his family. Find a fine field clover or alfalfa plant, and soak the ground around it with water until you make a very deep mud puddle. Then pull, loosening the root gently, so as to get as many rootlets as possible. Wash the earth away from the root in a tub of water. All over the root-fibres you will find funny little brown wart-like knots and swellings.

Those knots are the houses of little animals called bac-te′ria. This is how they help the plants. All kinds of plants need a food called nitrates. There is some in most soils, and some is supplied by animal manures that you often see spread on gardens in the spring. In the air is a great deal of gas called nitrogen. The leaves of plants cannot use that gas. They send it back to the roots. Clovers and other pod-seeded plants have these little animal friends that fasten themselves in colonies on the roots, and use that nitrogen gas to make nitrates. So those little swellings are really nitrate factories full of busy workers. They make more nitrates than the plants they grow on can use, and leave some in the soil for wheat and other crops. So, you see, the clovers are soil-makers, and bring good crops and good luck to the farmers.

If you see pussy prowling around a clover field, leave her alone. Pussy eats field mice. Field mice eat baby bumble bees. If the mice were so many that they ate all the bumble bees, the clover would have no help in making seeds. Then bossy cow would have no clover to eat, and couldn't make as good milk. And we wouldn't have as sweet yellow butter to put on our bread.

Isn't that just like the house that Jack built? Dear, dear, but this is a nice, mixed-up, friendly old world, where everybody helps everybody else, and has a fine time doing it.

Sometimes, clover will not grow in a field at all. Men who make a study of plants found out that this was because there were no nitrates in the soil, and no nitrate making bacteria to help the plants make them. So the farmer's department of our big country, in Washington, D. C., began to hatch bacteria in liquid baths. Cotton is soaked in this bath and dried. This cotton is sent to farmers who ask for it, together with some food the little animals like. The cotton and the food are put into a barrel of water. In a few days the water turns milky, and is then swarming with the little creatures.

The farmer lowers a sack full of clover, alfalfa, peas or bean seeds into the water, dries and sows them. The bacteria begin to grow as soon as the seeds do, and set up their little nitrate factories on the roots. If you can't grow sweet peas in your garden, or white clover on your lawn, ask Uncle Sam in Washington to help you. He will send you some of the cotton, and you can use the milky water for sprinkling.

It isn't a bit of use to sow these bacteria with any other kind of plants than pod-bearers. And here's another funny thing. When clovers and their cousins are grown in soil rich in nitrates, they do not take the trouble to make this plant food at all. You may pull up many a fine clover or alfalfa plant and find no swellings on the roots at all.

You have heard the story of Bruce and the spider, haven't you? No matter how many times the web is torn down the spider spins another one. Some animals will give up, if disturbed too often. So will some plants. The clovers are like spiders. They try, try again to grow seeds. If left alone they ripen their seeds from the first blossoms and the plant dies. But if clover is cut when in blossom, but before the seeds ripen, it will spring up and blossom again, and even the third time. Farmers can cut two and even three crops of clover from one field, in a single season. Then, if they let the seed ripen, the alfalfa and some clovers will re-seed the field, or spring up from the roots the next season.

It really seems as if those wise little clover heads might be nodding in the wind as if to say that they knew a thing or two, doesn't it?

# The Bonny Briar Bush

It was a little bird that told how the wild rose came to be growing in the wild garden.

There wasn't another wild rose anywhere in the neighborhood. Roses are something like human babies. They do not like the smoky air of cities. You can coax garden roses to bloom in front door yards and parks, but wild roses stay outside, where the air is pure and sweet.

When winter came, and the gray weed-stalks rustled their dry seed-cases in the wind, the rose seemed the only live thing in the waste place. Its thorny, leafless canes were a bright red-brown. Its scarlet seed-hips glowed like little coals of fire above the first November snow. The rose-hips were as big and heavy and red as the little apples of the hawthorn tree. And they were so firmly fastened to the woody stems that the wind could not loosen them. Some foolish robins, who had stayed in the north too long, made a breakfast of the rose-hips and started south for the winter.

Birds have perfect little mills of stomachs for grinding worms and seeds, but rose-hips are so thick and hard that it must take the birds days to digest them. The seeds inside are like little stones wrapped in spiny hairs, so they pass right through the birds unharmed, and are planted far away. In this way the wild rose has been scattered by birds over many parts of the northern world, from very cold countries almost to the hot tropics, and far up mountain sides. Some bird had dropped rose seed in that jungle of sturdy weeds in the city. It took root and grew there, because it happened to fall on a bit of soft, rich ground near a rotting stump of scrub oak. But it never grew very large or bore many blossoms.

The rose has a woody stem that grows, year after year, in rings, like a tree. Some people call it a rose-tree. But it is only a shrub or bush, the promise of a tree. The wild rose is often only a clump of separate, thorny canes. On them you can find the tiny leaf and flower buds in winter. And in the spring you can peel the thin, satiny bark away, and find the green layer of the new growth under it.

In March, when the buds begin to swell, put some branches of the wild rose in water, in a sunny window, and watch the leaves unfold. They are compound leaves of five, seven or even nine oval,

282

saw-notched leaflets. Where a rose leaf joins a stem, two ears or wings are set, giving it a broader, firmer hold. The under side of the leaf is furry, or even a little prickly along the mid-rib, and there are sharp thorns on trunk and branches.

Thorns are curious things. They start to be leaves or branches but get nipped, in some way, so they turn into thorns. They are very useful to roses. They help the slender canes catch on supports, and they frighten away some enemies. Little boys and girls would be sure to pull too many sweet roses if it wasn't for the scratchy thorns. Can you think of any other plants that have thorns? Thistles? No thistles have spines and prickles. A true thorn has wood and bark. Blackberry and raspberry briars have thorns. So have crabapple and hawthorn trees. Those plants, too, have five-petaled, rose-like, fragrant blossoms. Perhaps—but wait a minute. Don't think too fast!

The blossoms of the rose grow in clusters at the ends of the branches. You find there a bunch of hard green buds that seem to be the swollen ends of stems. The bud is solid where it joins the stem, but the covering of the tip is parted into five, thick, green, leaf-like scales that are folded around a hard center. Those scales are called sepals. As the bud swells, pink lines peep out between the sepals. Then, slowly, the sepals separate into five pointed lips of the solid, round flower cup below. They flare back and show five, broad, pink silk petals set in a fluttering rosette.

Just five in the wild rose! Once in a long, long time you may find ten petals, for you know there are some plants born with a genius for going up higher. The rose is so beautiful, and it has such a sweet smell, that it has been petted and fed and helped to grow better, in sheltered gardens, for hundreds of years. In every country it was just a little different, even when wild. It was a tiny shrub a few inches high, in far northern places, a tall bush or a long, trailing vine farther south. And it has been transplanted and the pollen crossed so many times, that it has been wonderfully changed. From the single pink, or white, or yellow blossom, the rose has grown into the many-petaled, many-tinted queen of the garden.

It was easier to improve the blossom of the wild rose because, just inside the circle of five petals is a little forest of pollen-tipped threads, around the five button-topped columns in the middle. The rose makes more pollen than is needed to grow seeds. It has no honey to give to bees and butterflies. It has its pretty color, its sweet perfume and its pollen to attract friendly visitors. These pollen threads are very ready to drop their yellow dust and broaden into petals. And they are just as ready to turn back again. If the seeds of the finest, double garden roses are planted, they sometimes forget all their long training, and go back to the single-petaled blossom and straggling canes of the wild rose. They have to be grown from cuttings to keep them tamed.

Left alone, Nature might never have made one of our double roses of the garden. She doesn't seem to care to make the *flower* better. All she thinks about is the seed. As the rose must depend upon birds to scatter her seeds, she tries to see how tempting she can make the fruit, so the birds will be sure to eat it. When the pink petals fall, the seed cup swells and closes its mouth, leaving those five sepal scales to turn dry and brown at the top of the red hip. The rose hip is too hard for some seed-eating birds to manage in their little insides, so one member of the rose family made the soft, sweet, seed-filled fruit of the blackberry. Another one made the raspberry.

Yes, those plants are cousins of the rose. They have the same bright-barked, thorny, woody stems; the same spiny, compound leaves, and the many five-petaled rosette flowers, with forests of pollen-tipped hairs in them. In the briar berries the blossoms are white and the pollen dark. Down in the grass Nature set the same white, rose-blossom on a creeping vine, and scattered the hard seeds on the outside of a sweet fruit, like stitches of yellow silk on a red satin cone—the strawberry!

Of course, no one knows which of all the rose family came first. Very likely it was the little yellow-flowered cinquefoil that looks so much like a wild strawberry. Besides making seeds it also grows by runners, that strike root at the joints. So does the strawberry. If raspberry and blackberry canes are bent over to the ground, they will often strike root, and start new plants. And branches of roses, and many of their cousins, can be grafted on other root stocks. So can the branches of orchard fruit trees be grafted.

How much the apple blossom looks like the wild rose. It has five pink petals set in a rosette. It has a little forest of pollen hairs, too. When the petals fall the seed case swells and closes at the top and leaves, at the flower end, five little dry, brown sepals. The leaves of the apple tree are furry on the under side, the bark of the tree is smooth and bright, and the wild apples—the hawthorns and crabapples have thorns. The apple tree is a very near cousin of the rose, nearer, very likely, than the strawberry. There are many varieties of wild apples in different countries—the Siberian crab-apple is a useful fruit in its wild state. Like the rose, the wild apple has been trained, fed, sheltered, transplanted, cross-pollinated and grafted, until there are now dozens of varieties of big juicy apples in our orchards. The pear and the quince are near cousins of the rose, too.

The wild plums and cherries are not so near. They have a single nut-like seed in a stony case. They grew, perhaps, in a round-about way, from the almond, and so did the peach and the apricot. A peach stone is pitted like the paper shell of the almond, and the peach seed is often mistaken for the nut of the bitter almond.

It is the rose that gave the name to the family. *Rosaceae* is the name. Isn't it pretty? It ought to be, for every member of the family makes the earth fragrant and cheerful with its bouquets of blossoms. The rose is so sweet, so innocent and beautiful that we borrow its name for little girls, as we do the blossoms of the violet and the lily. In Japan, where they grow orchard trees for the flowers, they often call little girls plum blossom and cherry blossom.

All members of the rose family are like the bonny briar bush in disliking the smoky air of cities. They grow best in the open country, under the wide, blue, sunny sky, in clean earth free from weeds, where birds build their nests and there is a pleasant hum of bees. And here is a secret very few people know. You can find the wild rose blossom in winter. Find a beautiful rosy apple. Cut it across the middle. Then cut a thin slice from one half and hold it up to the light. You will find the five rose petals there, very plainly marked, in the heart of the apple.

# The Story of Trees

## A Year in the Forest

Do you remember Eagle Heart, the little red American boy? His home was in the forest. We cannot find such a beautiful forest in our country today, as the one he lived in. No big tree had ever been cut down, except by the beaver dam-builders. The Indians had only stone hatchets. They used poles and bark to make their wigwams and canoes. For fires they used fallen trees and branches and dry brush. They were careful to put out their camp fires, so that very few forests were burned.

In the old world the woods had been cut over, and only the best timber and orchard trees replanted, for many hundreds of years. It was a very great wonder to white people who came to America, to see hickory, walnut and ash trees, oaks, maples, beeches, elms, poplars, willows, birches and wild fruit trees, flowering shrubs and vines, and even pines and other evergreen trees growing together, in the most natural and friendly way. In any bit of wild woodland, in any city park, and on village streets and lawns, you can find most of these trees, and some others that Eagle Heart never saw at all. White people brought the beautiful horse chestnut, and the tall, slim, Lombardy poplar and other trees, from their old homes.

How many of these trees do you know? Eagle Heart knew and loved all the trees in his forest home. Perhaps you know several of them in the summer, when the leaves are on, but he knew them in every season of the year. He knew their height, their color, their spread of limb. He knew their bark, their leaves, their flowers and fruits. He knew where each kind of tree liked best to grow, and what animals and birds and insects used it for a home. And he knew the forest as a whole, in all its seasonal changes.

After three hundred years of cutting down trees, we have begun to replant and protect them. Even the schools have a tree-planting or arbor day, so little citizens can help in the work of winning back our lost trees. The more you know about trees, the more you can help in this work. Don't you want to know and to love them as Eagle Heart knew and loved them? The first thing to do is to visit trees, and make some pictures of them with your little kodak eyes.

**RED MAPLE FLOWERS**

Photos, Mrs. L. W. Brownell

**RED MAPLE FRUIT**

**SILVER MAPLE FRUIT**

**PUSSY WILLOW FLOWERS**

PAPER BIRCH FRUIT

YELLOW BIRCH FLOWERS

Photos, Mrs. L. W. Brownell

WHITE BIRCH FLOWERS

WHITE BIRCH FRUIT

288

## ROSE AND APPLE BLOSSOMS

Apple blossoms and roses belong to the same family. Compare a wild rose blossom with an apple blossom and you will find they are similar in many ways. Apple trees will grow in higher altitudes than most fruit trees. They blossom later than cherry and pear trees, and so are not so likely to be damaged by night frosts in early spring.

# Spring: "Rockaby Babies"

Where do you look for flowers in the spring, and when? Why, on the ground, of course, and in late April or early May.

The Indian boy looked *up,* in March. He saw flowers much earlier than you do. The air is warmer than the ground in the early spring. Before the snow goes off the red maple lights the edges of the woods and the banks of streams with its blood-red blossoms. Against the cold, gray-blue sky of March the maples look redder than they really are. The flowers are so small, and so crumpled and bunched in little tufts on the sides of twigs, that you may think them only the first leaves. Frost nips a good many of them. Entire clusters fall to the ground, sometimes on the snow. You can easily find and study them.

You will find a number of tiny blossoms snuggled together, inside a raincoat of varnished brown scales lined with wool. The separate flowers are fairy cups, some with pollen pockets on little hairs, like clappers in bells, and other with eager arms or plumes stretched out asking for pollen. It takes both kinds of flowers to make the winged seed of the maple, and they both grow on the same tree. The bees get their first sweet breakfasts of the year from the ruby honey cups of the red maple.

A week or two later, the Indian boy looked for the flowers of the rock or sugar maple. They are not so easy to see, from the ground, for flowers and leaves come together, and both are a pale yellowish green. The flowers are not bunched, and each cup hangs by a hair-like thread. The whole tree has a feathery, spring-like look that tells everyone who knows anything at all that the sweet sap is running up. The tree pumps up thirty or forty gallons of water in flowering time. The silver maple flowers early, too. Its blossoms are in thick short tufts of greenish white, much the color of the leaves. The flowers of all the maples grow on the sides of the twigs. The leaf-buds are at the ends.

290

The snow is still trickling away in little icy streams when the first willow pussies come out for an airing. You will not find them on the big willow trees, but on bundles of knobby switches of willow shrubs that grow with their little webby root feet in the water. The bark is a brownish-green satin, with gummy, scale-covered buds set at regular spaces along the slender, leafless stems.

These scales open, and furry gray noses poke out to take note of the weather. If the sun is shining, the pussies slip right out and sit, as if with toes and tails under them, like so many Maltese kittens. You like to rub the silken pussies on your cheek, and you almost expect to hear them purr. But in a few days they swell and stretch and bristle, like kittens with their backs up about something, until every gray hair shows a grain of yellow pollen under it. Shake a twig and see the gold dust fly!

The big willow trees know better than to bloom so early, when Jack Frost nips foolish pussies. When the April sun is quite warm, the black willow takes the brown water-proof caps from its flower buds, and pushes out some catkin tails as scaly as pine cones. Each row of scales is dropped over the next lower one as neatly as the shingles on a church spire. They have no fur, for nobody needs fur in April. Under the scales are seed bottles with eggs in them, but no yellow pollen to feed them. Somewhere nearby, there is sure to be another black willow tree with no eggs, but with pollen catkins as yellow as gold. The bees visit both trees for honey, and so carry pollen to the eggs. The yellow tassels fall very soon, but the scaly ones stay on the trees awhile. By and by the seed babies under the scales get so big and downy that they tumble out of the nests and fly away.

All the catkin bearing trees—the willows, alders, birches and poplars, make these feathered seeds. In April and May, the woods are full of flying white flakes. One poplar is called the cottonwood because of the snow storm of downy seeds it set loose. The alders are mostly shrubs, growing with the willows along the waterways. Their scaly, worm-like catkins, that you can see in winter, swell into long feathery tassels of purple and gold. On the same bushes are little erect cone-catkins that bear the seeds. The birches like drier soil. You know these white-barked wood fairies, don't you? The birches are shy, and so are their blossoms. You have to lift the thin scales of their catkins to find the thinner scales under them and the hidden pollen. The tassel grows feathery, and the downy wood sprites of seeds seem to ripen and vanish in a day. The birds use the cottonwood and willow seeds to line their nests with down.

A great many trees flower in April, when the wild flowers in the ground are just poking little green cones through the warm blanket of last year's leaves. The pollen-making blossoms of the elms are little chimes of bells, yellowish or reddish green and, in some kinds, greenish purple. They have so many sturdy little yellow-tipped clappers that you almost expect to hear them ring. In the elm, as in nearly all forest trees, it takes two kinds of flowers, working together, to make seeds. So some of the blossoms of the elms have no clappers, but hairy arms that reach for pollen food. The wind brings it from other trees.

The elm seed is a round, notched and fringed and double-walled green scale, with the seed between two layers, just like the powder in a toy pistol cap. The seed hang in bunches, by inch-long hairs, until the wind tears them loose and scatters them. At the same time in May, the red maple drops its two-winged seeds. They look very much like the thumb screws that you use to tighten bolts, only, of course, they are thin and green.

Oak trees also have two kinds of flowers. One kind is a dwarf catkin or cone, with several double pockets full of gold-dust. The egg flower is a tiny pink knob. It sits away out on the end of the twig in a scaly cup, often snuggled up to a sister or two, like a little bump on a log. Its pink mouth is as wide open as a baby robin's when crying for worms. It wants that pollen? You see, it is a baby acorn. When it gets the pollen it swallows the food, shuts its mouth tight, turns green, and just sits there and grows all summer.

The acorn is really a kind of nut. And you might say that all of our forest nuts are made in much the same way as acorns. The chestnut seed-cone grows on the same twig as the pollen-catkin. As there are to be three nuts in one bur, it has three mouths to be fed with pollen, all set in one prickly cup.

The black walnut doesn't bloom until May. Its catkin has forty pockets of gold-dust, each one a sort of treasure shelf under a green scale. But the nut blossom is no bigger than a grain of wheat. You have to look sharply to find it. Two or three of them often grow together, on the tip of the branch, after the leaves come out. Small as they are, each has two mouths open for pollen. Why two, for one nut? Crack a walnut, hickory nut, an English walnut or a pecan. These nuts are in two, fat wrinkled leaves, with a woody partition between them. But they are joined across the middle like Siamese twins.

You can make a very close guess as to what the fruit of many trees will look like by studying the blossoms that hold the little eggs. You know the sweet, three-cornered little nuts of the beech tree, don't you? The squirrels know them. Three nuts are fitted together in the husk, so, in the egg blossom, which is just a tiny grain, there are three little, three-cornered mouths to be fed. The pollen blossom is a globe-shaped bell, with a dozen powder-tipped threads.

What would you think the blossom of the wild grape should look like? A many-branched cluster of flowers, for one thing. The flowers have five petals and five pollen threads, and a many-celled egg cup for the many seeds of the grape. But the flower petals do not flare open. They are almost closed into little grape shaped globes around the seed-making parts. The flower stalk, with ever so many branches and separate flowers on it, may be only an inch or two long, but it is a whole baby bunch of grapes.

Do you notice that the grape has both of its flowers, the seed cup and the pollen threads, set in one blossom? This is the first one of the kind we have found. The catkin bearers, the maples, the elms and all the nut trees have two kinds of flowers. One is a pollen maker that falls as soon as the yellow food is scattered. The other is an egg blossom that is fed, and stays on the tree awhile to ripen the seeds. In the grape, the two flowers are brought together, and set in a five-petaled cup, or ball.

The same is true of the wild crabapple and hawthorn trees of the woods. Plants with these united flowers are called crown-bearers. They are of a higher order than those that have to make two kinds of blossoms to grow seed. The crabapple blossom is so large that you can find out just how it is put together. The stem ends of all the parts are packed in a solid green cup that swells out on the end of the stalk. In that cup are little eggs in five nests. Growing up from the nests are five, hollow, white columns with moist, spongy buttons on top. Around these columns is circle after circle of yellow-tipped pollen threads, as many as thirty of them. And outside of these is the rosette of five pink petals, held up by the five green sepal scales, or flaring lips of the egg cup.

Bees brush the yellow pollen on the white columns, and the grains of gold-dust send hair-like roots down to the little seed eggs.

Then the petals fall, the seed cup closes and swells, the sepals dry into five little brown scales at the flower end. The apple grows big and juicy, and ripens brown seeds in five satin-lined nests in the heart.

The crown-bearers do not use their own pollen, but exchange it with flowers on other trees of the same kind. Such a flutter of silken, scented petticoats; such a buzzing of bees and hovering of butterflies as goes on in those huge bouquets of pink and white! Besides what we call the wild fruit trees—there are the honey locusts, the horse chestnut and buckeye trees, and many crown-flowering shrubs, in American forests.

The honey locusts hang out long clusters of pink butterfly blossoms, like nosegays of little sweet peas. The honey bees go frantic with delight over them. In June, the horse chestnut gives its second surprise party of the year. Don't miss that for anything. You can find these handsome trees in lawns, parks and along village streets.

The swollen cone of the horse chestnut flower bud is in the heart of a cluster of five-fingered leaves, often a foot long and broad. The big white blossoms are on erect, many-branched spikes, so they form a giant bouquet. Each blossom is a fluttery, ruffy cup, penciled and dotted with purple and yellow. They are deep honey pots, into which bees tumble, head first, jostling the hanging pollen pockets and bumping into seed column tips. When the petals fall in a little snow storm, the seed grow into husks, into dark brown nuts, much like big, flattened acorns. The horse chestnut is a foreign cousin of the American buckeye tree. The Ohio buckeye that gives its name to the state, has clusters of smaller greenish flowers, and the sweet buckeye long, narrow, yellow flowers in green cups.

Under the lowest limbs of the tall forest trees are the flowering shrubs. The wild briar berries have clusters of white rose-like blossoms. There are bouquets of white-flowered dogwoods, pink sprays of red-bud, and yellow torches of the spice bush. The elder shrubs have showy parasols of tiny white blossoms, and the laurel makes banks and drifts of pink snow on rough hillsides.

This is the forest in flower, as the Indian boy knew it. Do you wonder that he loved it? If you learn to know it and love it as he did, it will call you out every day from March to June.

CHESTNUT FLOWERS

Photos, Mrs. L. W. Brownell

ELM FRUIT

HONEY LOCUST FLOWERS

DOGWOOD FLOWERS

BUR OAK FRUIT

WHITE OAK FLOWERS

Photos, Mrs. L. W. Brownell

RED OAK FLOWERS

RED OAK FRUIT

# Summer: "In the Tree Tops"

Summer is the leafy season.  But the time to begin to study leaves is in the early spring.  On nearly all trees the leaf comes as soon as the blossom falls.  The first leaves are very small, and they are not green but pink, red, yellow, gray or white.  They have been wrapped up in bed clothes all winter.  It takes several days of warm sunshine for them to turn green and to grow up.  The leaf of the red maple tree, true to its name, is red.  On the sugar maple it is a yellow-green, on the silver maple a shining green-white.  When they grow to full size these maple leaves all have much the same form.  In different members of a plant family there is a resemblance, as in a human family.  You can learn to call each one by its "given," as well as by its family name, by looking out for the differences.

When you see a tree with a leaf that would lie in a three to five inch circle, but that is cut down part way into five lobes, you would be safe in thinking that tree a maple.  The lobes of the red maple are sharply notched and parted.  In the sugar or rock maple, the leaf lobes and partings are more rounded.  It is a darker, smoother leaf, too, and grows more thickly on an evenly balanced, round-headed tree.  The red maple has straggling branches, and the leaves are thin so light sifts through them, giving the tree an airier look than any other maple.

The leaf of the silver maple is smaller, a sage green above, a cottony white below.  It does not sift light, but seems to reflect it like a mirrow, as the white underside turns up in every breeze.  There are other maples, but these are the best known.  The leaves of all trees and of low plants, too, are alike in being brighter and smoother on the upper side.  The underside is paler and rougher, and the veins stand out more plainly.  This is because the upper side is a sort of rain and dust coat and sun-umbrella, for the breathing pores underneath.  It is the lower side of a leaf that is the more interesting to study under a microscope.

All of the willows have long, slender leaves.  Each leaf is a narrow, thin, delicately veined blade that grows by itself, and alternately, along a slender stem, making a sort of feathered branch.  The pussy willow leaves are a bright green.  The black willow leaf is broader, saw-notched, and it tapers toward both stem and tip like a canoe.  It is bright green above and silvery underneath.  The leaf of the white willow is a gray green lined with silver, and it droops from yellow stems.  The crack willow, whose twigs snap so easily, has a green leaf lined with a waxy coating.  The weeping willow has long, sad, gray "weeping" leaves.

The leaves of the alders are darker and broader than those of the willows, and the undersides are hairy.  The poplars all have broad, heart-shaped leaves of emerald green satin, many of them silvery underneath.  They are always in motion, so they shimmer in the sun in quite a dazzling way.  The tall, slim, Lombardy poplars seem robed in dark green, flowing satin.

Except the maples and willows, very likely you know oak trees best.  The oak leaf is very irregularly shaped, like the oak tree.  It is a long, oval or pear-shaped leaf, usually narrowest at the stem end, and is deeply notched and lobed.  It is a strong, tough leaf as glossy above as if varnished, and rough underneath, with woody veins standing out like a net-work of cords.  The scarlet, the red and the black oaks have about five, sharply notched lobes with broad partings, and each lobe is often notched again.  The white oak has seven or nine narrow, rounded lobes, with very deep rounded partings cut down almost to the midrib.  The bur oak has five or seven broad round lobes and narrow partings.  In the swamp oak the leaf is deeply and irregularly scalloped.  The chestnut oak leaf is oval with shallow scallops, and the smaller live oak leaf has wavy edges.

The oaks ring all the changes from many sharp, almost spine-tipped lobes to wavy edges.  And they are very puzzling, for they are not all alike even on one tree, nor in different seasons.  The best way to be sure of an oak tree is to study the acorns.  Oaks can be as tricky as they like about leaves, but they stick each to its own pattern, in making acorns.  So, in the fall, when the acorns drop, you can study the oaks again.

After these tantalizing oak leaves, it is always such a comfort to turn to the American elm.  That tree can always be depended upon to make a certain leaf.  Along its high branches, that curve over in great plumes, the elm sets an oval or egg-shaped leaf about three inches long, narrowest at the tip and just a little pointed.  The elm leaf grows singly, on opposite sides of twigs, each a little advanced beyond the last, and making a neat, feathered spray.  The leaf is strong, saw-notched, short stemmed and firmly set, smooth above, rough underneath.  From the midrib the veins slant upward, making

evenly spaced broad V's, about a quarter of an inch apart from stem
to tip. You might think these veins were laid off with a ruler. Isn't
that a satisfactory kind of leaf? You could almost draw it without
seeing it, couldn't you?

The leaf of the beech tree is something like that of the elm,
but thinner, softer, often fringed as well as saw-notched along the
edges, and it is irregularly net-veined, not strongly feather-veined
like the elm. The tree, too, is so different that you could not mistake them. The beech is a broad, low-branching tree, leafed all over
as heavily as the maples.

The orchard fruit trees, wild and tame, all have rose-like leaves.
Apple tree leaves are a soft green above, lighter and furry underneath. They grow in tufts around the fruit and along the stems.
The cherry leaf is smaller, darker, brighter, and more blade-like than
the apple leaf. The foliage of the pear tree is larger and thicker;
of a peach a long, slender, bright green blade like a very large, rather
curly willow leaf. On the thorny canes of the briar berries are broad,
spiny compound leaves that tell very plainly their kinship to the
rose. In open spaces of the woods, the wild grape spreads its tent
of broad, deep lobed and toothed leaves. They are very glossy and
dark green above, hairy and pale underneath. And among them
are curling tendrils and bunched clusters of little green fruit.

In every forest you will see several trees that have what are
called pinnate leaves. Such leaves have three or more pairs of leaflets set on opposite sides of a central stem, with a single leaf at the
tip. So in a pinnate leaf, there are always an odd number of leaflets,
five or seven in the rose, about nine in the leaf of the white ash tree.
This is a beautiful shade tree, of hard wood, ranking with the rock
maple and the elm. The leaf is quite nine or ten inches long, and
the leaflets along oval blades very bright and clean. The mountain
ash, or rowan tree, has as long a leaf and a greater number of
narrow leaflets, giving the tree a feathery, almost fern-like look. The
honey locust, too, has this feathered leaf of many drooping leaflets.

Many of the nut trees have these beautiful drooping pinnate
leaves. The black walnut is hung all over its high crown with long
plum-like leaves with from seventeen to twenty-five slender leaflets.
The leaf of the butternut, or white walnut tree, has from seven to
nine. The horse chestnut, buckeye and hickory trees have palmate
leaves. That is, the broad oval leaflets are all set around the tip
of a common leaf stem, spreading in a circle, like the ribs of a palm

leaf fan. The largest, middle leaflet of the horse chestnut leaf is often ten or twelve inches long, and four or five wide.

It is a wonderful thing to see a horse chestnut burst into leaf in April. This tree has thick stems and big, scaly leaf-buds like little pine cones. The outer scales are brown, and water-and-frost-proofed with gum. Inside is layer after layer of green scales each lapping over the next. Inside of all these is a tender, pink, leaf-bud baby, snuggled in a blanket of fleecy white wool. Now watch and see one of these undone, for all the leaves of all trees come out in much the same way. You can study Mother Nature's way of wrapping up and taking out her leaf-bud babies in the horse chestnut best, because its buds are so large. One by one the cover scales are turned back as the baby stretches too big for its cradle. Then, on a warm day, five crumpled pink toes wriggle through the fleecy blanket. Suddenly, the bed clothes are kicked off, the pink toes spread into five leaflets and the whole tree tumbles, green in a day, into the sunlight. But it takes the leaves days and days to grow up.

The paper or canoe birches have the prettiest fairy-like leaf in the world! It is a broad oval, three or four inches long, with finely toothed edges. The pointed tip is often curved over a little, in a graceful, tricksy way. This is a way many leaves have of being a little out of balance. It you fold any leaf along the midrib you will find the two sides are never exactly alike. This is just as it is in the faces of little boys and girls. One cheek has the dimple, one eyebrow is lifted or eyelid drooped more than the other. It is these little things that keep any two faces, even of twins, from being exactly like any other, and give every face what we call character, or individuality.

The birch leaf has this little tilt at the tip, now on one side, now on the other, with a little hollow cut out below it. A thin, fluttery, transparent leaf, scantily scattered over the lace-like twigs of the slender white-barked trees, it glances like a butterfly and sifts sunlight. A group of birches always have a dryad, wood-fairy look. Step softly when you come upon them in some shy retreat in a forest. They look as if a snapping twig might startle them into taking flight.

# Autumn: "When the Wind Blows"

What is it the magician says in fairy stories, when he makes the most surprising things happen?

"Presto, change!" and he claps his hands.

Jack Frost is this wonder worker of the forest. After a still, sharp night in October, a hundred things seem to have happened all at once. The ground is white with frozen dew. The trees are great torches of gold and red. They blaze all the brighter because the sky is veiled with a violet haze.

It is the maples that first light up our woods with these flickering fires. No country of the Old World has trees that make such a wonderful color show as our maples. Their leaves are never of one tint, but are mottled and shaded, from lemon yellow to orange, flame-red and crimson. You know the thin-leafed red maple sifts sunlight. To look up through one, in the fall, is like looking through a splendid stained glass window of a church.

The oaks show no yellow, and the leaves are of a strong solid color. But different varieties of oaks give them a range of all the reds from scarlet to wine, and then add warm browns and bronze greens. The elms and beeches are in russet yellows, the birches and poplars pure gold, the nut trees yellow. On every brook the willow leaves float like little fleets of sunny canoes. The fairy crafts drift down stream, swirl over eddies and go under.

Below the boughs of the tall trees, all these colors are repeated in the shrubs and vines. The sumac is a burning bush with torch-cones of seeds. The broad leaves of the grape vine turn to bronze. The berry briars are dark as the wine oaks. The big, smooth sassafras leaves are mottled in orange and flame, like the maples. There are notes of purple in the clusters of wild grapes, in the leaves of the alders and some of the ashes; and of scarlet in the seed hips of roses, the clustered berries of the mountain ash and of the bittersweet vine. Below all these the foot-high seedlings of the forest show the colors of the parent trees, among the brown of frost-bitten ferns and fallen leaves.

There is no hurry about anything. The autumn trees often take three or four weeks of Indian summer to strip their boughs for winter. The leaves drift down, silently, like great colored butterflies. Whole troupes of them dance in little gusts of wind. On frosty nights the nuts drop with soft patterings. Squirrels slip, brown and gray shadows, over the bright carpets, laying in their winter stores. The song birds take their last meals of seeds and cocoon babies and **fly** southward.

October is the time to study the fruits of forest trees. Many of the trees—the willows, poplars, elms and red maples drop their seeds in the spring. The rock maple keeps its seed until frost, and so do all the nut trees and the wild orchard fruits. All the maple seeds have two thin, flat, green wings, like a thumb screw, an inch or more across. In the thickened bases of the two wings, two seeds lie coiled. You can peel away the thin, paper-like covering and find them. And you can learn how they begin to grow by pulling up the smallest seedlings of the red maples.

Acorns lie thick under the oak trees. They will tell you the names of the parent trees. But keep very still and the squirrels will tell you some things. The gray and brown squirrels and the little striped chipmunks will pass some acorns by, but will pick up others eagerly and scamper away with them. Up the trees they go, or into hollow logs or holes in the ground, to their hidden store-rooms. They like the sweet acorns of the white, the chestnut and the live oaks. They have to be very hungry before they eat the bitter nuts of the black, the red and the bur oaks. How can they tell them apart?

Very likely all acorns look alike to you. They all have a shiny, brown shell with a white "eye" where they grew fast to the cups. The acorn of the white oak has a very rough, mossy cup much shorter than the pointed nut. The bur oak is often called the over-cup oak because its mossy, fringed cup covers quite two-thirds of the round acorn. In the live oak of our southern states, the cup tapers back to the twig, broadens at the top and almost encloses the acorn. The red oak has a shallow cup, more like a saucer, the scaly ring just clasping the long oval acorn. The scarlet oak acorn is top shaped, with a point for spinning, and is half covered with a shaggy cap of a cup, like a tam-o-shanter. There are other oaks, with acorns that are still different, but these are the best known.

Chestnuts are very near relatives of the oaks. The cups are closed burs, very stiff and woody, with prickly thorns. You have to let Jack Frost open them for you. He can split them into four leaves lined with brown velvet, and make you a present of three dark brown, flattened nuts with silky tails. They are very sweet when roasted by a winter fire. The squirrel is out before you are after chestnuts. Did you know he often peels his nuts, stripping the horny shell away, before storing it in his high pantry. He puts away chinquapins, those tiny American cousins of the chestnuts. He likes the little three-cornered, thin-shelled beechnuts that grow, three together, in a prickly bur. He gathers hazel nuts, too, picking them from the flaring, clustered husks that grow on low bushes.

Would you think the squirrels could manage the hard shelled walnuts, butternuts and hickory nuts? The black walnut has a thick stony, wrinkled, black shell, and it is buried in a tough green husk with no partings. You have to let these husks dry a little and turn brown. Then you pound them off. They stain your fingers brown. The butternut is a white walnut. Our grandmothers used to dye homespun cloth brown with butternut husks. The hickory nut is smooth, white and a thinner shelled and sweeter kerneled nut than its cousins. It pops out of a thick, four-parted, smooth husk. The pecan, a very high bred southern cousin of the walnut, leaves its wide-open husk on the tree awhile, when the nut falls. It has a thin, pale, smooth, oval shell and a fine, sweet kernel.

You can easily prove that all these nuts, and the English walnut, are very near relations by cracking them. All of them have two fat, wrinkled seed-leaves, joined through a hole in the middle of a thin partition wall. The leaves are not twin nuts. They are just the two parts of one seed. You know beans and pease seed have two leaves that split when the plant begins to grow. So have the acorn, the chestnut, the buckeye, and the seeds of all plants with net-veined leaves. The forest nuts are the only ones that build partition walls between their seed leaves that the writer ever found. Do you know of any others?

How did the nuts get their hard shells, and their tough or prickly or mossy husks and cups? Just as the apple got its rosy skin, its sweet pulp and its horn-lined seed nests. The shell of a nut is like the seed nest of the apple. It is the hardened covering of the baby egg in the blossom. The cup or husk of the acorn, is really the twig on which the blossom grew. A plant can grow stem and root and bark and leaf and flower, all so very different. So it isn't hard to take a twig bud and turn it into a thorn on the rose, or a tendril on the grape vine, or a cup or husk on a nut tree. Nature is always turning these slight-of-hand tricks, making the most unexpected things out of anything she happens to have in stock.

For two or three weeks our autumn woods are draped in splendor, and dropping their ripened fruits for squirrels and birds and little boys and girls to find.   Then come a gale of wind and cold rains. Suddenly, the trees are bare, the birds are gone, the squirrels asleep in their cosy store-rooms.   The baby leaves and branches and blossoms for next year are tucked up snugly in tiny brown buds, all over the trees.   You can find them in early winter, just above the scaly marks left by the leaves that have fallen.   Every one of them is a little prize package, rain-and-frost-proofed in spicy gums and fleecy blankets.

Isn't it wonderful that these tender babies, some no bigger than grains of wheat, will be safe and warm even when the ice is thick on the rivers and ponds?   Winds that break off great limbs of trees and almost blow you off your feet, will merely rock these babies in their cradles.   And under the blankets of leaves and snow, the fallen seeds will lie asleep, as snugly as Johnny Bear in his cave.   The first warm days of spring they will wake up, yawn so wide that they will split their shells, stretch, their leaf-arms up to the sun, and dig their root-toes into the soft earth.

# Winter: "The Cradles Will Rock"

Who says there is no use in going to the forests again until spring? What a funny mistake! It's worth while going if only for the pictures in black and white. Many people, who know a great deal about art, like black and white pictures best. They like drawings in crayon, charcoal and ink; prints from etched plates, and fine photographs. The woods, in winter, against gray skies and snowy earth, are delicate etchings. The boy with a kodak, then, is lucky. He can make a whole album of pictures.

Every tree has a character of its own, just as every person has. Don't you know the members of your family and many friends by the way they stand and sit, and carry their heads, and swing their arms when walking? You don't always need to see their faces. You can learn to know trees in that way too. Their character seems to come out more sharply when they have no soft, colored drapery of leaves to hide them.

The oak tree looks as if its shape were wrought of iron. No two oaks are alike, but all look as if hammered out on some giant forge. Its stout trunk, covered with deeply furrowed black bark, is rooted like a rock. Often it is buttressed, or braced, by great ridges that slope away to outstanding roots. It supports a great weight of thick limbs, irregular and crooked. Clear up to the knotted twigs, and tough brown leaves that often hang on all winter, the oak has a stubborn look. It dares the winter winds to do their worst. And it looks so old, so wise, such a scarred hero of a thousand fights. The old Norse sea kings and the brave English once worshiped the oak tree. It gave them ship timbers that could stand the strain of wind and waves. Many ancient peoples thought dryads, or wood spirits, lived in oak trees.

The elm tree was believed to bless and protect a church or household. There have been many wonderful stories written about the elm. Its black trunk, with the bark in deep, vertical ridges, often springs forty feet in the air, straight as a pine, before it branches. Then, from the top, the long limbs sweep, like plumes from a vase. A double row of them makes a high arch across a very wide street. It was often planted for a lucky birth tree when a baby was born. The baby grew up before the elm did, but the tree lived long after

305

# CAN YOU TELL THE TREES BY THEIR BARK AND

Tree         Bark, Leaf, Fruit

WHITE OAK

Tree         Bark, Leaf, Fruit

CHESTNUT

Tree         Bark, Leaf, Fruit

SYCAMORE

Tree         Bark, Leaves, Fruit

SHELLBARK HICKORY

Tree         Bark, Branch with Fruit

RED CEDAR

Tree         Bark and Leaves

AMERICAN ELM

PHOTOS BY U. S. FOREST SERVICE

# HOW THE CLOTHES and SHAPES OF TREES DIFFER?

Tree        Bark, Leaves, Bloom

HOLLY

Tree        Bark, Leaves, Fruit

BLACK WALNUT

Tree        Bark, Needles, Fruit

SHORTLEAF PINE

Tree        Bark, Leaves, Fruit

SUGAR MAPLE

Tree        Bark, Needles, Fruit

BALSAM FIR

Tree        Bark, Needles, Fruit

WHITE SPRUCE

he was gone. His children and grandchildren played under it while it was still a young tree. Elms and oaks often live for two or three hundred years and get their names into history.

Isn't it wonderful that trees keep a record of their birthdays? Every year's growth is a thin layer of green that, as it hardens into wood, is plainly marked in a ring. The rings are bound together with rays like wheel spokes. When lumber is sawed and polished, the ring and ray marks come out in wavy lines, in delicate pencilings, in curls and "eyes", and color bands, very true to type in nearly all trees. So, in a chair or floor or door casing, you can learn to know the different woods. Grown people know many of these woods in houses and furniture. They know just what each kind of tree is good for.

The Indians knew a great deal about woods, although they could not cut down trees. "Give me of your bark, oh birch tree," sang Hiawatha. He wanted the white, unbroken bark of the big, paper birch tree to cover his canoe. "Give me of your wood, oh ash tree," he sang. He used the tough saplings of the white ash for the frame of his canoe and for his hunting bow. He knew the best fire-woods, too. He knew that a hard beech log would hold fire all night, that birch splinters made the best kindling, that pine-knots blazed up for story telling, that wild apple wood glowed with rosy flames like its own pink blossoms.

But we are forgetting our winter pictures in black and white. There are other trees with white, or silvery gray bark as well as the birches. Some willows and poplars, the silver maple and the syca-more, a kind of maple or plane tree, have them. And one birch has a yellow bark. You can always tell the birches in winter by the short, brown or dark gray cross-markings on the bark, and by the slender branches and twigs. The willows have many small, drooping twigs but large branches. They often have long, horizontal roots that push the earth up in ridges, and a little forest of switch-like shoots around their feet. The poplars are much like the willows, but their branches are more erect, often growing in so close to the shaft-like trunk as to make these the slenderest trees, except the pines. Switch-like shoots grow about the poplars, and even on the trunks.

In the winter the barks of orchard fruit trees are warm reds and browns and purplish grays, very bright and clean, like wild rose canes. The trunk of an old apple tree may be gray and scaly, but the higher branches and twigs are bright. It has a low, rounded head. Its stout branches spring from a short trunk, making that comfortable "crotch" where you like to sit with a story book in the summer. The crabapple is small, thorny, flat-topped, a twisted witch of a tree. The pear is tall, slim, with a few thick limbs growing upward and close together. The cherry is wine-red. Its outer bark easily peels in circular bands.

The black walnut tree has a towering trunk that branches high in a beautiful crown. Its bark is as black as the oak and elm, and sharply ridged like the shell of its nut. The butternut or white walnut has a grayish bark and high, horizontal branches. The hickory is a tall, spreading tree with a gray bark that breaks away in long strips. For this reason it is often called the shag bark. The twigs are a warm, yellowish brown, with big varnished leaf buds.

The beech tree has low-hung, wide, spreading branches. Its trunk is a smooth bluish-gray column. Nothing that grows under the beech gets enough sunlight, so the ground is often quite bare. The beech, too, like many heavy trees, braces itself with horizontal roots. It is the best umbrella in the world, in a storm, and it is thought to be the safest shelter, for it is seldom or never struck by lightning.

Bare maples are always graceful. The rock maple is a sturdy, compact tree, with its smooth trunk and rounded head. The red maple has a free, bold way of branching like its five-notched leaf.

Winter is the time of the year for finding bird's nests, for the owners no longer need them. The oriole often hangs its purse of a nest, seventy-five feet in the air, from the limb of an elm. Robins and blue birds are fond of apple trees and maples. Little wood owls like the hollows of oaks. The crow picks out a lofty perch in a cotton-wood or pine tree to survey this interesting world. You can find holes the woodpeckers have drilled to drag out grubs, and cocoons tucked away in the ridges of the bark. They hold the baby butter-flies waiting for spring. You can tell, too, if a tree is injured or dying. Fungi, or toad stool growths of white or orange fluted ridges, creeping thread moulds, and dry rot around hollows, mean trouble, and decay.

Sometimes, when the Indian boy lay in his wigwam, on a still, cold, winter night, he heard the trees crack. He could not have known what had happened. But now, when sound trees are cut up for lumber, they are often found cracked, across the middle or around a growth ring. The frost does not harm the smallest leaf-bud baby in its cradle, but it often grips and breaks the hearts of big trees.

Winter is the best time for studying the cone-bearers. Perhaps you call all of these trees pines. Many people do. Only one of their family is a pine, and you would never pick that one out for a Christmas tree. It has long, stiff, needle-like leaves that grow in clusters of from two to five. The clusters grow so close together that they spread in fan-like sprays. The pines, of which there are several varieties, have upright cones of thick, over-lapping, woody scales.

Pines, spruces, firs and hemlocks are alike in having cones and needle-like leaves. Most of them have tall, tapering stems, like ships' masts and telegraph poles. The spruces and firs make the prettiest Christmas trees. The spruce has inch-long needles that bristle all around the stem. In the fir, the needles are flat. They grow on only two sides of the stem, and they slant upward. Sometimes the under side of the leaves is pale and shining. Then it is called the silver fir. The cones of the two trees are much alike, long, slender, with thin, close-set scales. But the spruce cone droops, while the fir cone stands erect. Hemlock needles are short and flat, too, but they lie straight out like the fronds of a feather. The hemlock cones are shorter, with bristling, parted scales. All of these trees have a spicy, balsam-like smell that is very pleasant.

The cedars are very different from the needle-leafed trees. The tiny, flattened, or spiny leaves overlap each other, making scaly or mossy stems. The flat-leafed arbor vitae trees and shrubs are cedars. So are the round-stemmed cypresses, the junipers with their purple berries instead of cones, the gnarly yew-trees with their red or violet seed berries, and the giant redwoods of California. Much like the cedars are the club-mossed larches or tamaracks, that grow in swampy places. Some of the larches and cypresses drop their leaves in the fall.

The cone-bearers put out new leaves in the spring, after their blossoms, dropping the leaves from the older, inner parts of the tree, leaving them quite bare, and strewing the ground with brown needles. All the branches and twigs are tipped with tender green tassels and new leaves. Away up on the tip of the tallest pine is a long green feather. The Indians have a wonderful story about that. When a young chief was turned into a pine tree by some bit of magic, he was allowed to keep his eagle feather.

There the feathered tip of the pine waves proudly today, above all the trees of the forest.

# The Fly Tells Its Story

## Insects

"Were you speaking of me? Here I am."

A very dignified little visitor, about a quarter of an inch long, drops "out of the nowhere" in the most surprising way! But she is very polite about ringing a little buzzing door bell to let you know she is coming. "Buzz-z-zip! I'm Mrs. Musca Domestica!"

What a name for such a little creature! One of the capital letters of it would almost cover her, and the length of it would make a nice distance for an evening stroll.

"It's just Latin for 'house fly'," she says. "Don't you think I deserve it? I come into the house whenever you leave the screen door open. I'm neighborly and don't wait to be invited. I'm very fond of human society. You have such nice things to eat. But you are not very friendly," she added reproachfully. "Actually, I've had the door shut in my face, and been 'shoo-ed' out like a hen."

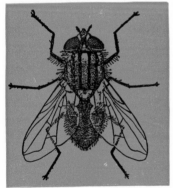

A house fly magnified.

"Well, you're not very clean, you know. You go to dirty places, and you don't wipe your feet."

"I would if I had a door-mat, I would, indeed. I wash my face and brush my clothes oftener than you do. Just watch me."

There she sits at a respectful distance, rubbing her little front hairy legs together vigorously. Then she balances herself on the other four, and rubs the hindlegs. When the middle pair are cleaned, she drags a leg across her mouth to wet it, and washes her face like a cat. Finally she flutters her silver gauzy wings to shake the dust off. As a delicate hint she nibbles at a clean plate.

"Don't human people ask their visitors if they care for refreshments? Thank you! A grain of sugar is my favorite lunch. You may watch me eat, if you won't come too near."

She has no legs to spare for picking up food; but she has a little mouth that drops like an elephant's trunk. Out of that mouth comes a dew-drop of liquid to make syrup of the grain of sugar. The knob on the end of the mouth parts, and the two lips spread out flat over that drop. She stands there licking with a little rasp of a tongue blissfully until she has sucked it all up. Then she wipes her mouth with her foot, and cleans herself all over again.

"I have another name. It's Diptera. That means two-winged. My family is very important. It's the biggest one on earth, with thousands of members. You can always know a Diptera by the two wings. Most insects have four. One of my cousins is very musical, but I am sorry to say, he is also a blood-sucker. If he shows any

Tsetse Fly, found in Africa. Its bite kills cattle, horses and dogs.

fondness for people, it's because he likes to bite them. His name is mosquito. The horse- or gad-fly can make horses jump and even run away. The Hessian fly stings wheat. The saw fly lays her eggs on rose blossoms. The tsetse fly kills cattle sometimes; the gall fly stings plants and makes galls grow on them. And there are gnats

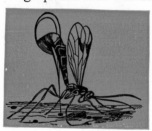

and midges. They come in swarms. Did you ever hear of 'a plague of flies?' "

"Yes, indeed, and 'the fly in the ointment.' You spoil a good many things. Your whole family seems to be a nuisance."

"Not all. The dragon-fly and ichneumon fly are useful. And I don't see what you have against me! I can't bite or sting, and I eat very little, compared with some

Ichneumon Fly: is useful because it destroys insects which injure trees and shrubs.

people I could mention. To be sure, I have little tickly hairs on my feet and scrapers on my tongue, and they make people nervous. And I like to wake lazy people up in the morning. No one can sleep after daylight when I'm around. If you had only one summer to live, you'd want to get up early and make the most of every day.

"It's pretty hard to catch me, too. I have several thousand little flat eyes in the two in my head. They're like the facets of a diamond, only ever so many more of them. I can feel, and I can smell food with these two feather plumes on my head.

"No, indeed, I *never* fold my wings, when I sit down, as foolish moths do. I keep them ready for business. Aren't they pretty? I make them of silver gauze, and paint them with bronze and purple. Do you notice cream-tinted scales behind them? Those are balancers. If I didn't have them I'd tumble head over heels when I tried to fly. I can tilt my head, too. It is set right down on my shoulders, on a kind of pivot.

"No, I never have dyspepsia, thank you! You see, I make syrup or broth out of everything I eat. The good goes into a little mill, with spiny teeth, to be chewed and mixed with something to digest it. Then it goes into a little bag of a stomach. I can tell you how not to have lung troubles, too. Don't have any lungs. I breathe through holes in my skin like the leaves on the trees. I fill little air bladders and pass the air back to blood vessels.

"If you really want to know how wonderfully I am made you ought to have a glass that would magnify me a hundred times. I

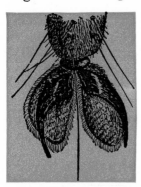

A fly's foot magnified.

have three silver girdles across my chest, or thorax, a yellow band on my abdomen and some golden spots. All six of my legs are fastened to the thorax. But if there is one thing I am vain of it's my feet. Just look at them. The legs are jointed, and on the last joint of each is a pair of claws like a lobster's. But they close over a pad or cushion covered with knobby hairs. All those hairs are sticky, and cling to things. Really, the smoother you make your walls the better I like them. A gold picture frame, or a nice white gas globe just suits me for an evening stroll, or a bed to sleep on, upside down. But every thing sticks to those feet! I can't keep them clean, although I wipe them on every bit of bread or food you leave out for door-mats."

"Ah, so that's why you bring typhoid fever into the house, naughty fly!"

"Well!" with a little bristle of wings. "No wonder! You ought to see where I have to bring up my babies. I can't carry them around, all legs and no arms as I am, now can I? I have to lay my eggs in warm moist places around stables and in garbage cans, or

2—3

they never would hatch or have anything to eat. You never see those eggs. They are dull, chalky seed-looking, little things, buried in smelly places. They hatch out into little white squirmy larvae in twenty-four hours, and eat that decaying stuff. I wouldn't touch it myself! I like the good things on human tables. In less than a week those babies grow as long as I, and shut themselves up in brown cradles.

"Asleep? You wouldn't think so, from all the things that happen in a week's time. Why, they make themselves all over, from little white, crawly, unpleasant grubs into—"

"Beautiful little winged creatures like their mother?"

"Not just at once. When they push the front ends of their cradles off and crawl out, their wings are very small and soft and baggy, and cling close to their sides. Those infant flies are pale and sickly looking. You wouldn't think them likely to live. And they breathe by puffing out their foreheads in the most comical way. I assure you I don't always know my own children.

"Do I have many children? Oh, quite a few. I never keep any account of them. I lay nearly a hundred eggs at a time and four times in a season. In just fourteen days after an egg is laid it is hatched, eats, grows, makes a cradle, comes out and is a full-grown fly ready to lay eggs itself. I shouldn't wonder if I would be several times a great grandmother before I die. I'm not saying it to brag. It's a trait of the whole Diptera family."

"Mercy, no wonder there are so many of you!" Mrs. Musca Domestica rubbed her clothes brush legs together, thoughtfully, and washed her face for the third time.

"There are not so many house flies as there used to be. We really threaten to die out. People don't leave as many piles of refuse about for us to lay eggs in. They scald their garbage cans, put lime in plumbing traps, and actually wash stable floors with hose. There are screen doors and windows everywhere. If we do get into a house, there is sticky paper to catch us. In some houses there isn't a crumb about. I really wonder such stingy people don't starve themselves. We have other troubles, too. Most of us die of a kind of fungus that paralyzes us, in the fall. Haven't you seen us sitting around, unable to move, with gray bands around our bodies? A few of us do manage to creep into cracks of warm houses, and go to sleep until spring. And there is—

"Did you say spiders? ? ? Good-by! ! !"

## PROTECTIVE MIMICRY AMONG INSECTS

Nature has provided that many insects and animals have the shape or color of the things around them. Thus they are not easily seen. This is important for two reasons. First, their enemies can not find them easily. Secondly, they can creep up undetected on their prey. Can you find three butterflies on the branches in the center of the page? Can you find another long-legged, leaflike insect on the branch at the upper right? Can you find the worm in the center of the page, looking like a stem? Can you find the bug on the bark at the right side of the picture? And note how the long insect at the bottom of the page looks like a little branch with twigs. What other kinds of protective mimicry can you find on the page? In the woods and fields you will find many other examples. You will find green bugs in the grass, brown bugs on the ground, and brown chipmunks with dark stripes down their backs which merge with the trees and leaves. When the little chameleon lizard is on a brown background he changes to brown, and when on a green background he changes to green.

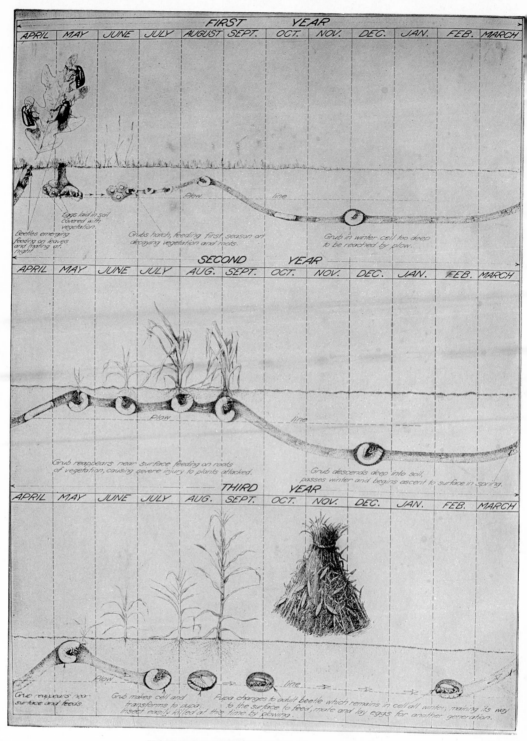

## HOW TO DESTROY THE WHITE GRUB

Many insects do great damage to crops. They often have long and curious life-histories, which scientists have studied so that we may know how and when we may most easily kill these insects. The destructive May beetle or June bug has a curious life-history, lasting three yars. It begins as an egg laid in the ground in the spring. The egg soon hatches into a larva or white grub, eats roots during the summer and spends the winter deep in the ground, below the frost line so it will not be killed by freezing. The next spring it crawls near the surface and spends the summer eating roots, particularly of corn, again going deep in the ground when winter comes. The third spring it again eats corn roots, changes into a pupa in July and August, when it is near the surface and may easily be killed by plowing in the autumn. If it is not killed, it becomes a flying beetle the next spring, and lays eggs which hatch into another generation of crop-killers.

# Mrs. Garden Spider "At Home"

Mrs. Garden Spider won't come to see you and buzz by the hour. If you go to see her she'll tell you plainly that she doesn't care for society. It takes all her time to build her house, earn her living, and bring up her babies. She isn't asking favors of anyone, and she'll be obliged to you if you won't stand around and scare flies away.

But she makes such a pretty house that you feel like going anyhow. It's a gossamer wheel of a curtain. You can find it in almost any garden, stretched across a fence corner, or between the low branches of stout shrubs. You won't often see the little gray and brown mistress of it. That house is merely a sun-parlor of a net, spread in the open for the unwary fly. The lady of the house is of such a retiring nature that she prefers to live in a dark tunnel den behind the parlor. Stand out of sight—and remember Madame has from two to eight eyes in her head, and can see all around the compass—and fling a bit of dry leaf on the web. She darts out. She views the leaf with disgust, thinking the wind has played a trick on her. Very likely she will push it overboard, for she keeps her house clean and shining.

Any time a hard rain or wind comes along the pretty house may be wrecked. Then you may watch Mrs. Spider build it again. She has to do it before breakfast, too, or go hungry. Get an opera glass, if you can, and watch her at a distance. She sits out on a leaf or twig or fence post, looking over the building site. She isn't easy to follow, being the color of dead wood, half an inch long, with eight threadlike legs, and darting movements.

She drops, or jumps, from one support to another, paying out a tiny gray silk cable behind her, and fastening it wherever she can. Soon she has an irregular space inclosed. Do you know how fine those lines are? You would have to lay four or five thousand of them side by side, to make a ribbon an inch wide. You can see her run around those lines and pull them with her hind foot to test their strength. If one breaks she spins another.

She jumps, or drops, across the space, carrying a line, and fastens it to the farther side. She runs back to the middle, doubling the line as she goes, and jumps across at right angles. Soon, she has her space cut into four equal parts, as neatly as mother cuts an

317

apple pie. Then she cuts each piece in two, once and again, making eight, then sixteen pieces. Those are the spokes for the wheel web. The many crossings make a stout hub. She tests the spokes, pulling on each one and running over them. She has three claws, and fine-toothed bristle combs on her hind feet. May be she combs the snarls out and brushes away dust.

Back she goes to the hub and weaves a spiral line, crossing the spokes and gluing the joints. She does it much as your mother makes

Spider and its web.

a spider wheel in lace work. After a few wide turns, she makes the crossing circles closer together, because the spokes flare farther apart. She doesn't fill in all the space out to her foundation lines. Some building sites are larger than others. She takes the best one she can find, but her web is always about the same size.

Finished? No, indeed. When men build houses they first put up the frame work, then cheap scaffolding to stand on. Mrs. Spider sets up scaffolding to walk on. She starts back from the outside edge of the wheel. This time she uses a much better silk. It is studded with little sticky beads. You heard Mrs. House Fly say she liked smooth things to walk on, didn't you? Gummy spider webs tangle in the hairs on her feet, and hold her for an instant. Mrs. Spider knows that very well. Her web is a very good sticky fly paper. As she travels back to the hub, she cuts the scaffolding away. Then she makes a silk den behind the web, and connects the web and the den with a telephone, or door bell wire, that she keeps her foot on. That web is stretched like a drum-head. When a fly drops on it, it vibrates.

Wonderful, isn't it? And it didn't take Mrs. Spider more than an hour to make it. If it is destroyed she seems to have plenty of material to build another. It really is *Mrs.* Spider who does all this work. You will nearly always find her living alone. Mr. Spider is very much smaller than she is, and he is not a worker. As the female bees do all the work, and drive the drones or males out of the hives, or even kill them, so Mrs. Spider barely tolerates her mate and even eats him if other food is scarce. She builds her own house, catches her own food, looks after her babies, and lives all alone in a busy solitude.

A long, long time ago the work of this clever spinner and weaver was looked upon as pure magic. The Greeks made a wonder story about her. The spider was a maiden named Arachne (A-rak'ne). In a contest of spinning and weaving she proved herself better than the wise goddess Athe'na. To punish her for daring to be more clever than a goddess, Arachne was turned into a spider, and told to spend the rest of her days making her wonderful web. Unable to talk, Arachne kept the secret of her spinning until men made microscopes. Now, it seems as if this little creature could always have told men how to make spinning frames to turn cotton, silk, wool and flax fibres into yarn.

At the rear end of her abdomen are from two to eight little pin-head knobs, in pairs. These are spinnerets. Each one is covered with hollow bristles. Altogether there may be a thousand of them. From each one comes a hair of liquid silk. They all flow, or are twisted together into one thread. The spider seems able to expel, or shoot out, the silk and fasten it to any support, and to use the lengthening cable to propel herself. Haven't you seen house-spiders let themselves down from ceilings by these silk cords? Once started a web thread seems to be pulled from the spinner as fast as she travels.

The spider is not an insect, as are the fly, the ant, the bee and butterfly. She has eight legs, while insects have but six. Her body is in two parts instead of three. Her legs are jointed like a lobster's, and like the lobster and crab she is a fierce fighter, and hunter. If a leg is torn off in a fight she is usually able to grow another one. She has no wings to fly, but is a regular acrobat, doing high jumps, and long leaps, and tight-rope walking and cliff-climbing up smooth walls. You see, she has eight legs, each one with seven joints. Seven times eight are fifty-six joints, and all of them are as limber as a trapeze performer's The spider's jaws are steel traps with biting teeth, and behind them are little poison sacs. Few spiders could hurt you seriously, but their bites paralyze flies and other small insects.

From the two to eight little eyes in her head, to the same number of spinnerets in her tail, from the deadly jaws to the sensitive, clawed and bristled and padded foot, the spider is a wonderful little creature. She is as clean as Mrs. Fly, washing her face and brushing her hairy body and legs vigorously. She keeps her web clean and every thread mended. And she cares for her babies as tenderly as a mother bird.

Did you ever see a garden spider moving along slowly, dragging a little gray silk ball with her last pair of legs? That is the cradle she makes of silk for her eggs. It isn't fastened to her. When at home she keeps it in the den, or hangs it on a nearby twig. But when she travels she takes it with her, although it hampers her, and makes it much easier for a toad or frog or bird to snap her up. If she drops that ball she hunts for it frantically. Her babies are not hatched out as greedy little grubs, but as little specks of spiders. That is quite unlike any insect. And Mrs. Spider carries her babies on her back. They just swarm all around her like chickens around a hen. She must have to feed them at first, much as a robin feeds its nestlings.

Don't kill spiders in gardens. They eat insects, oh, a great number of them, for they are big eaters. Nearly all insects are harmful, or their grub babies are, living, as they do, on plants. The spiders' wheel and sheet webs and tunnel dens, are very wonderful. The little creatures are as patient, skillful and industrious as bees and ants. They neither use nor destroy anything useful, and they help us grow flowers and vegetables, by eating the flies and moths that lay their eggs on plants.

# Gulliver Man and his Lilliputian Enemies

Once upon a time a baby was born. It was a very, very small baby, and almost too feeble to move. Yet, the very first day of its life, it ate two hundred times its own weight. As long as it lived it ate as greedily as that. It was nearly all mouth and stomach. Every day or two it outgrew its own skin. The skin split down the back, the baby crawled out in a new and larger skin, and went right on eating. It seemed never to sleep. In a few weeks it changed its skin five times. When it was grown up it was ten thousand times as big as when it was born.

What a monster! If this were a human baby, it would have eaten a pile of food as big as a ton of coal the first day. And, when fully grown, it would have weighed one hundred thousand pounds. Is this a giant story, like that of the Brob'ding-nag'ians in Gulliver's Travels? No, it's a "really, truly" story, but the monster babies are more like the Lilliputians. They were the tiny people, who swarmed all over Gulliver when he was asleep, and tied him with thin threads. Our Lilliputian enemies are caterpillars and grubs. They are hatched from little eggs, and grow to be hundreds of times as big as when born.

"Once upon a time" is right now, and all the time. You can find these monster babies on every lawn, in every garden and park and farm, on the grass, on small plants and big trees; buried in soft fruits and hard grains, and in tunnels they have bored in roots and stems and tree trunks. You can see their fathers and mothers flying in the air, too. They are beautiful butterflies and moths, shiny beetles and gauzy-winged flies. How pretty they are, and they don't seem to be doing any harm at all.

So long as they have wings few insects eat much, and most of them live only a short time. But the females are busy laying eggs. That little gray moth, half an inch across the wings, that you see hovering over the pink apple blossoms, lays an egg that hatches into the apple worm. The fat white grub eats its way through, spoils the apple and crawls out. It spins a rough cocoon, just the color of the tree, and under a scale of bark. There it lies all winter, coming out as a moth, in the spring, to lay more eggs in the blossoms, to spoil more apples.

All insects go through this larva stage. Then they do nothing but eat. Bees feed their babies with honey, so they do no harm at all, and are very useful to us. But most insects die when they have laid their eggs, and they leave their greedy babies to eat plants that men work so hard to grow. They always lay the eggs where the larvae can find their favorite food, and they lay hundreds and even thousands of eggs, most of them too small for you to see.

When the eggs of butterflies, moths and flies hatch, they come out as caterpillars with six legs, hairy or smooth worm-like bodies and chewing mouths. The larvae of beetles are usually footless grubs. Some of them look much like the parent insects, but are less active. They all begin to eat ravenously. Inside there is little but stomach and material for making cocoons. Leaf-eaters grow to full size in a few weeks. Orchard fruit and nut eaters stay in the fruits until they fall. The larvae of some boring beetles live in the wood of trees for two or three years. They honey-comb solid trees with little tunnels.

When grown to full size the larvae of all insects spin cocoons or make horny or papery cases. Some roll up in leaves, using a very little silk to close the openings. They use the hairs from their own bodies, sometimes, to mix with silk, or with plant fibres. These cocoons nestle in the ridges of bark, hang from stems or leaves, or lie in the ground. Cocoons are often so nearly the color and texture of the thing they are fastened to, that you may look at hundreds of them and never see them at all.

There is no living plant or animal that these little creatures do not prey upon. As insects they sting, suck blood and sometimes kill the higher animals. But it is as grubs and caterpillars that they eat and injure millions of dollars worth of grains and fruits and garden crops every year.

Wheat has three insect enemies—the chinch bug, the Hessian fly and the wheat midge. When ground into flour the meal worm often hatches out and makes it unfit for use. On the potato plant is the Colorado beetle that eats the leaves, so they cannot make plant food. The cabbage head

Hessian Fly which causes great damage to wheat.

is burrowed into by the larva of the cabbage moth. Big green caterpillars feed on the tomato, and the grape vines. A moth makes wormy apples and pears, but the curculio, a weevil beetle, punctures the skins of plums, cherries and peaches, and pushes an egg down to the stone. The currant worm strips the bush fruits of leaves. The slug of the saw fly destroys roses, and little, green, plant-lice, or aphides, suck the juices of rose bushes, fruit trees and hop vines.

Cotton plants have three enemies—the cotton-boll weevil, the cotton worm, hatched from a moth egg, and the cotton stainer, a little red beetle. The chief enemy of corn is the cut worm. The army worms march from field to field, millions strong, destroying

Cotton-boll weevil; first figure showing insect at rest and second showing wing-covers lifted and wings extended for flight.

grasslands. Grasshoppers come in clouds and leave bare fields behind them. On the bark of fruit trees a leech of an insect sucks unseen, under the black speck disc of the San José scale. The tree dies and the pest spreads through an orchard. The tent caterpillars often take entire limbs of fruit and shade trees. They weave a cob-web tent over a big colony of squirming leaf-eaters.

The number of species, or kinds of insects, is far, far beyond all other living creatures put together. Some scientists say there may be a million species. They all lay countless eggs. One scientist says that a young cherry tree may have ten million plant-lice on it. In one year the codling moth has put worms into ten million dollars worth of apples, and the Hessian fly has destroyed one hundred million dollars worth of wheat in our country. All the insect pests put together cause a loss on our farm crops, orchard fruits and garden products of more than two billion dollars in some years.

Isn't it a wonder they leave anything at all for human beings and the higher animals to eat? Farmers and gardeners fight these enemies all the time. They spray plants and trees with poisons. They plow land in the fall, to turn up buried cocoons to the frost. They plant trap-strips to catch the larvae, and burn the strips. In gardens they pick off grubs and caterpillars by hand. They cut down trees and limbs and burn them. All the year around these enemies, too small, often, to be seen, too high to be reached, too hidden in the earth, in the fruits, the bark, the hearts and roots of plants, to be found, are fought. But all that human beings can do, is to keep them in check—sometimes. And sometimes men can only look on, quite helpless, and see fields laid waste. Don't you think farmers must often feel as Gulliver did, when he was bound by those swarms of five or six inch high Lilliputians?

If men had no help in fighting these billions of enemies they would lose the battle. But these greedy little creatures have enemies of their own, that live among them and prey upon them. These enemies of the insects are our friends. Do you know any of them?

Birds? Oh, yes, of course, all the song birds. We will tell you about our bird friends in another story. But there are some useful insects, too, that live on their kind, and a few other humble creatures that you may think of as pests. Perhaps, not knowing, you may have killed some of them. You ought to know all these friends so you can protect them, for we need all the help we can get in growing useful plants and animals.

# Pygmy Friends that Fly and Hop and Creep

Lions and tigers are such terrible beasts that you are very glad they live in circus menageries, park zoos and far-away jungles. As for dragons, very likely they never lived at all, except in story books, along with mermaids and jobberwocks. But insects could tell you quite a different story. In their world, up in the air, down on the ground, in earth dens and even in the water, are beasts of prey that devour them. The very names of some of them are enough to frighten their victims into spasms. There are dragon flies, ant lions, tiger beetles and spiders. But some of them have quite innocent names, such as frog, toad and lady-bird.

Wouldn't mosquitoes and flies and gnats be indignant, if they knew that we think the dragon fly beautiful? But it is as beautiful as any butterfly, and in its darting, skimming flight it is as swift and graceful as a swallow. It really is the swallow of the insect world. It catches and eats its food on the wing, and it eats nothing but flying creatures smaller than itself. It hunts its small game over ponds and ditches, swamps and marshy shores, just where insects breed by millions. Very likely you call these pretty friends of ours snake feeders and devil's darning needles, but they are too busy feeding themselves to feed snakes, and they can't sting or bite you or sew up your ears, at all. They are as harmless as humming birds.

There are several varieties of dragon flies, darners and damsel flies, but they are all insect feeders. They have very long, slender, stiff bodies of dazzling metal colors, in steel blue, purple, green bronze, copper and silver white. Their four long, narrow, silver-gauze wings are beautifully veined, and are often spotted with white or brown or amber. Their big, jewel eyes stand out from their heads and glitter like automobile lamps. And they have regular snapping-turtle mouths.

On very hot midsummer days there often seems to be nothing on the wing but these glitter-winged dragons of the air, and their swarms of little victims. Some of them skurry to shelter in the water weeds if a cloud blows up, but others love to frolic with the wind, and will even go out over white-capped waves on the sea shore. If food is scarce on the water, some of them will go up into meadows and orchards and get a lunch of codling moths and weevils.

325

The green-bodied darner even ventures on the lawns, and eats house flies and mosquitoes there.

When dragon flies alight, which isn't often, for they seem tireless, they keep their wings outspread. The damsel flies fold their slender wings down their darning-needle backs, in the shyest way, as if they didn't want to be noticed. Their name comes from the French —demoiselle—which means young lady. One of the damsel flies is so gray and modest that it is called marsh nun.

Dragon Fly. It has no sting and is harmless to man. It feeds on insects which it catches while on the wing.

All these are insect feeders, both in the winged and in the larva stage. They lay their eggs on the water, or on the stems of water plants. The larvae are not worms or grubs, but imperfect insects something like grasshoppers. They are called nymphs. But you will never see them. They live in the mud and on stems in the water, and they eat tadpole mosquitoes, and other water larva.

There is another insect something like the dragon fly that looks as if it might sting. It has a long, wire-like tail that it can curl over its back and poke into a hole in a tree. This is the ichneumon fly (ik-noo'mon). It often stands on the bark of a tree exactly like a woodpecker, so motionless that you can snapshot it with a kodak. It has very long, jointed legs and feelers, and one kind has a body that flares out behind like a brass horn. Some people think the ichneumon fly bores those holes in trees. But the hole is made by some boring beetle. At the bottom of each hole is a grub that feeds on the wood. The body of that soft, fat grub is just the place the ichneumon fly likes to lay an egg in. Then, when the baby hatches, it eats the grub. The fly will go all over a tree and poke its flexible wire egg-layer into countless holes. This clever creature eats very little, but spends most of its time laying eggs in the larvae of moths, butterflies and beetles.

Sometimes you may see an insect that looks like a small dragon fly, but that flaps its four gauzy wings, in flying. It lays eggs in tiny sand deserts in the woods, on river banks and sea shores. An innocent looking flier it is, but its larva is a true beast of prey—the cunning, flesh-eating ant-lion. The egg hatches into a clumsy, humped, bug-like creature, with spiny hairs to which wet sand sticks. It has six digging legs, and jaws like a mouse trap. It makes a round pit about as big as would be made by pressing the bottom of a small teacup into the sand. When an ant or other little creeper runs over the edge of the pit, it just naturally slides down hill. Before it can climb out again it is snapped up by the half buried ant-lion.

Another sand-dweller with a lair is the tiger beetle. It is brave in a shiny armor of copper, golden green, sand color or pea green with white spots, and is striped and spotted like a tiger or leopard. Its jaws are long, horny, hooked and toothed, and they shut together like the blades of scissors. The larvae of the tiger beetles dig pits in which they lie, mouth and eyes out, snapping up all small insects that come their way.

Did you ever catch a pretty red, black-spotted lady-bird beetle on a rose bush, and say:

Lady-bird, lady-bird, fly away home.
Your house is on fire, your children will burn!

It fairly leaped in wild alarm, when you let it go. Lady-birds cannot walk well, so they are easily captured, but they can fly. There are black lady-birds with red or yellow spots, too. Do you know why you can find them on rose bushes and fruit trees? They eat those little soft green plant lice, or aphides, that swarm on certain plants. In England, gardeners hunt for these neat insects to put into flower gardens, orchards and hop fields. If they couldn't get these little friends in any other way, very likely they'd be willing to pay for them.

LADY-BIRD

French gardeners really do pay four and five cents a piece for ugly, warty, little hop toads. Toads eat almost anything—red spiders, flies, wasps, caterpillars and moths. And they just dote on cabbage and green salad worms. Nothing touches the toad. He has no teeth to bite, or claws on his webby feet to fight with, or a stinger. But he has glands behind his jewel-like eyes with which he can make a dreadful smell. This liquid doesn't cause warts as some people think, but it gives the toad a nice wide field of lonesome-ness. He is a night prowler, coming out at dusk. In the daytime he sits in a shady place taking a mouthful of air at a gulp, now and then.

The toad, like his water cousin, the frog, has a long tongue, fastened to the front of his jaw. It unrolls, darts out like lighting, catches an insect on a gummy tip, and snaps back quicker than a wink. A toad can clear a house of cockroaches, and a few in a garden will give you more sound vegetables and fewer worms. Tree toads are useful in forests and orchards, and frogs in ponds and swamps. The garden spider is useful, too. (See Mrs. GARDEN SPIDER "AT HOME.")

There is another very humble, helpless little friend that you should not harm. This is the smooth, pinkish-brown worm that you dig for fish bait. It is a true worm, and not a caterpillar or larva of an insect. Its real name is earth-worm. It eats earth for the water and decaying vegetables, but every bit that it eats passes through its soft body, and is powdered and enriched so it will grow plants better.

After a hard rain you may see sidewalks strewn with their dead bodies. They cannot live without moisture, but too much rain often drowns them out of their burrows. If a living worm is touched it shrinks to half its six or eight inches of length, which shows that the little blind creature can feel, and be afraid. Then you can see that its body is made up of ring muscles. And under a magnifying glass you can find tiny hook-like feet, and a sharp gimlet of a boring nose. The nose bores through and through the soil. One worm, it is said, can turn up a quart of finely powdered earth in a summer. And it must turn up many insect eggs and cocoons to eat, or else it would starve. Earth worms is one sign of good soil. When the soil is naturally poor, or is worn out by bad farming, there will be few earthworms in it or none at all.

By Ewing Galloway, N. Y.

## The Grasshopper—a Great Destroyer

Every year grasshoppers destroy millions of dollars' worth of field crops, garden truck and cattle feed. In parts of our country, they sometimes move in vast droves which destroy crops completely.

## The Japanese Beetle—Another Destroyer

This insect destroys everything it touches in plant life. It was first seen in the United States in 1916 in New Jersey. Here some are shown eating the leaves of a peach tree. They are most destructive in July and August.

Courtesy of The American Museum of Natural History

From Ewing Galloway, N. Y.

SPRAYING A DDT PREPARATION FROM AN AIRPLANE
TO KILL MOSQUITOES

A FEMALE MOSQUITO—THE ONE
THAT BITES

A FEMALE CLOTHES MOTH
LAYING EGGS

330

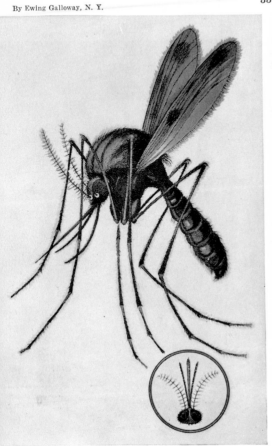

# Bees

"A swarm of bees in May
Is worth a load of hay.
A swarm of bees in June
Is worth a silver spoon.
But a swarm of bees in July
Is not worth a fly."

Before the world had sugar, honey was an important article of food. While not so highly valued today, how many boys and girls enjoy wheat cakes and waffles with honey.

The bee is an insect related to wasps and ants. There are many kinds of bees and they are found in all parts of the world.

The social bees including the bumblebee and honeybee, are the best known. The honeybee was brought to this country from Europe over three hundred years ago. The escaping swarms filled the forests with wild bees.

In the bee family we find queens, workers and drones. The queens and workers have stingers connected with poison sacs but the drones have no stingers. Each kind is produced in a different kind of cell. The cell in which the queen is reared is quite large. The cell of the drone is larger than that in which the worker is reared. It is possible for the workers to enlarge a cell and by changing the food to royal jelly cause the young grub to develop into a queen. When more than one queen hatches at the same time it means trouble. The queen that succeeds in stinging the other queens to death is mistress in the bee home. The queen lays eggs in large numbers, placing in different cells those she wants for workers, drones and new queens.

The workers do all the work of the hive. They gather the honey, bee glue and pollen, which is made into bee-bread to feed the young bees. They clean the hive, form the wax, build the comb and care for the young.

The formation of wax is very interesting. Some of the workers stuff themselves with honey and remain quiet for about twenty-four hours, after which the wax comes out as little plates from the wax pockets on the under side of the body. About twenty-one pounds of honey are used to make one pound of wax. The cells are six-sided. In building, the workers begin at the top and build downwards, leaving some spaces for passage ways. Some of the cells are for honey, others for eggs.

When the hive becomes too crowded, thousands will leave the hive led by the old queen. The first swarm usually leaves in June. The new queen is left in possession of the hive. A second and third swarming sometimes takes place. The swarms usually light on the limb of a tree, hanging like a bag. The bee-keeper is always watching for swarms and when they light he stuns them with smoke and puts them into a hive.

The bee has a long hairy tongue, spoon-shaped at the end to get the honey from the flowers. When not in use, the tongue is folded back beneath its head. Some of the honey taken up is eaten by the bee, some is stored in the honey-sac at the large end of the abdomen. This honey and a yellow dust from the flowers, called pollen are taken home. On the fourth joint of each hind leg is a pollen basket. As the bee enters the flowers, the pollen sticks to its legs and body and is later collected by the bee and put into the pollen basket.

The "busy bees" not only are carriers and honey-makers but they sometimes stop to feed a hungry relative from their store. When they meet they cross antennae or feelers to greet each other. Then the hungry one puts out its long tongue and draws honey from the mouth of the other.

A bee can see well. In proportion to its size, the bee has more eye space than the owl, two great compound eyes and on top of its head three small eyes. No wonder it can make a bee-line for a certain place.

Without the antennae or feelers, the bee would be lost. They serve as nose and ears as well as feelers.

A bee is very clean, is always cleaning itself with its legs which are brush and comb. The hives are kept clean too. Fresh air is fanned into the hives with the wings and the bad air is fanned out.

The bee has many enemies. There are robber bees to be fought, the bee moth must be kept from entering the hive and laying eggs. The larvae from the eggs will destroy both honey and comb. Birds will eat bees and bears will eat both honey and honeybee.

When the honey season is over and food is scarce, the workers kill the drones, the drone grubs and eggs. They will have that many less mouths to feed during the winter. The egg laying season for the queen is over. The other bees gather around the queen to keep warm and all is quiet in the family until the warm days of spring. Then the queen begins to lay eggs again and the life in the bee hive starts anew.

# LET'S LOOK INSIDE A BEEHIVE

The picture shows parts of two empty, unsealed honeycombs containing rows of six-sided cells, formed by bees to hold their honey and eggs. There is a set of cells on each of the two sides of the honeycomb. They are separated in the midddle of the comb. It is a marvel of nature that bees make a six sided cell, which is the best shape to combine strength, storage space, and economy in use of wax. If you will look closely through the center of any cell in this picture, you will see the point of meeting of three sides of three cells on the other side of the honeycomb. This form of construction greatly strengthens the whole comb.

## HONEYCOMB CELLS

When a swarm of bees begins to keep house in a new hive their first task is to manufacture wax out of which to make the comb. After eating all the honey possible they remain quiet for about 24 hours. Then the wax appears in these wax pockets that you see in the picture (greatly enlarged). Now some of them climb to the top of the hive and lay the foundation of the comb, and the making of it proceeds rapidly. Although a bee must eat 21 pounds of honey to make one pound of wax, each pound of wax will make 35,000 honeycomb cells.

## HOW BEES MAKE WAX

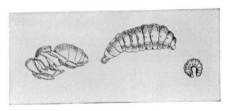

Pupa        Larva

Bees' eggs are about one-twelfth of an inch in length, and bluish white. In three days they hatch into little worm-like creatures, called larvae. They lie curled up in their cells, and are fed by the workers for five days. The workers then seal up the cells, very much as your mother tucks you in bed at night. Each larvae then spins a cocoon in twelve days and changes into a pupa. About a day later it emerges from its cell a perfect little bee.

## QUEEN ATTENDED BY WORKERS

The queen is treated with reverent courtesy and attention. When she moves about she is attended by a body guard, as seen in the picture. They feed her with honey and bee-bread.

# Bees

WORKER          QUEEN          DRONE

The queen may lay 100,000 eggs a year in empty honeycomb cells. The eggs hatch into larvae in three days. Most of the larvae are fed beebread, a bitter food made of pollen, which causes them to become workers. But a few of the larvae, hatched in special, larger cells, are fed rich royal jelly, which turns them into queens. Some other larvae, also hatched in larger cells, become the drones or fathers.

There are from 30,000 to 70,000 bees in a colony or hive. To produce a pound of honey, 80,000 beeloads of nectar are needed. A worker flies an average of one and one-half miles for a load. It sips the nectar from the flowers with its long, spoon-shaped tongue, and stores it in a bag in its throat. The worker also collects pollen, which it rubs into tiny balls and puts them in the pollen baskets on its hind legs, shown in the picture at left. When full of nectar and pollen, the worker flies back to the hive to make beebread of the pollen and to store the nectar, mixed with secretions from its body, in the honeycomb cells. The bees then work over the nectar, fanning it and modifying it into honey.

Honey Bee, Showing Full Pollen Basket on Hind Legs.

THE AMERICAN, OR BALD, EAGLE

**BLUE GROUSE (ABOVE) AND RUFFED GROUSE (BELOW)**

These are among the finest of the game birds. So swift is the ruffed grouse and so clever at dodging that he is not an easy target, and would be hard to exterminate were it not for the clearing away of the woodlands. The blue grouse is a Western bird with much the same habits as the Eastern ruffed grouse.

# The Story of Birds

## A Bird-Lover's Outdoor Aviary

This is the story of one of these old-time bird-lovers and his bird-haunted garden. He was a country doctor. He lived in a village in the Middle West, in a small white house with green shutters. In his large garden he had many beautiful trees, and the finest flowers and fruits and vegetables in the town, although he never seemed to take any more pains with them than did his neighbors. People said he was lucky, or had the knack of growing things. But the wise doctor only smiled and said:

"I have all my little feathered friends to help me." Few people understood just what he meant by that.

As the years went by, and wild birds became fewer, the doctor's garden was almost the only place in the town where many of them nested. Then people went to the doctor's house, to see and to hear the birds they had driven from their own door yards. The dearest treat the doctor kept for his little human friends, was to invite a few of them at a time to a sunrise concert on his vine-covered side porch. There, as still as little mice, they could listen to the bird songs, look through the doctor's big field-glass, and watch the happy singers at work or play. Now and then, the quietest child of all was allowed to peep into a big knot-hole in a fence post, and look at Mother Blue-bird sitting on her eggs.

That is the way in which one little girl learned to know and to love our wild song birds. Don't you want to go into the doctor's garden, and watch the birds as they come north in the spring? You can learn to know them by their songs and colors, their nests and babies. You can learn how they helped their good friend grow flowers and fruits and vegetables. And you can learn how he made them understand that they were wanted, and would be protected. If you know all these things you, too, can have the wild song birds for summer visitors wherever you live. They will come to farms and into sheltered gardens of houses in large towns, and into the parks of the very largest cities.

GOLDFINCH

ROSE-BREASTED
GROSBEAK

CARDINAL

INDIGO BUNTING

CHIPPING SPARROW

SONG SPARROW

TOWHEE

SCARLET TANAGER

BROWN THRASHER

WOOD THRUSH

BLUEBIRD

CATBIRD

VEERY

OVENBIRD

REDSTART

BARN SWALLOW

WHITE-BREASTED
NUTHATCH

TUFTED TITMOUSE

| RED-HEADED WOODPECKER | YELLOW-BELLIED SAPSUCKER | FLICKER |

| RED-WINGED BLACKBIRD | BOBOLINK | MEADOWLARK |

| STARLING | ORCHARD ORIOLE | COWBIRD |

ROBIN

When Mr. Robin comes, a little later than the blue-birds, he wears a smart new spring suit of brown, with a gay, red vest. He welcomes his little mate with a happy, mellow song. "Chirp, chirp," she answers faintly from the grass. "I'm rather tired from the journey, dear." "Oh, cheer-up, cheer-up!" he answers. Down he drops to her side, and perks his knowing little head to this side and that, as if to say: "I think I hear a worm!" Suddenly he stabs the ground with his bill, braces his stout legs, gives a jerk and up comes a fat grub for Mrs. Robin's wedding breakfast. Up to a low branch he flies and sings her another song of pride and joy.

All the male birds have a love song for their mates. Both birds have call notes, and harsh alarm notes to warn of danger, and to frighten away enemies. And they have talking tones. Mates will often flit about near each other, and exchange remarks. Very likely they are just talking about the weather, or the food supply, or their neighbors. You can spend a whole summer watching one family of birds, and learn something new every day.

If ever you do that take a thrush for first choice. The robin, the bluebird, the brown thrasher and the mocking bird are thrushes. Nearly all the thrushes have beautiful manners and sweet singing voices. The mockingbird is one of the greatest singers. He is all our own, too, for he is not found in any country of the Old World. He nests in our warm southern states. But once in a great while he comes north.

When the mockingbird begins to sing he springs or bounds upward, as if too happy to stay on the earth. The mockingbird is as long as the robin, but more slender. In color he is rather sober—gray above, with dark brown wings and tail that are tipped and lined with white. When the moon is full he often sings all night long. The only other bird that does this is the Old World nightingale. Our great poet, Longfellow, describes

MOCKING BIRD

the mocking bird's song in Evangeline:

"Then, from a neighboring thicket, the mocking bird, wildest of singers,
Shook from his little throat such a flood of delirious music,
That the whole air, and the woods, and the waters, seemed silent to listen."

Besides his own song he mocks all the other birds. He warbles and chirps and whistles; he twitters and trills, so you might think all the birds were holding concert when he sings.

The mocker's nearest rival in the garden was a red-brown-backed cousin, with a brown-spotted vest of cream color. Sometimes he is called the brown thrasher, from the way he thrashes his tail about. And he is called the brown mocker, too. One thing he does is to mock himself. He perches on a lofty branch of a tree to sing.

When the song is finished he seems to say: "I wonder if I could do that again." And he does it; exactly as he did it before. The English poet Browning has noticed it:

"That's the wise thrush, who sings each song twice over,
As if you might think he never could re-capture
The first, wild, careless rapture."

Besides his own song, "twice over," the brown thrush sings choice bits from a dozen other birds' songs, one after the other. "Hear me! Hear me!" he trills: "I can sing this, and this and this. Oh, the joy of it—under the blue—in the sweet wind—swinging. Don't you wish—you could do it? Try, try, try, yes you can, truly, truly!" Such a little cataract of melody, to fall from the high branch of an elm.

The catbird is a mocker, too. He is a thrush who can sing a pretty song when he wants to. But he is a saucy fellow. He caws like a crow and meows like a cat, to scare his timid neighbors into spasms, and to waken Rob Roy from his nap. Then he laughs at the joke. Do you know Mr. Catbird? He is quite a dandy, in a coat of London smoke and a pearl vest. He has a rusty-red tail that he jerks about when he sings. He skulks under bushes, and pounces on his creeping prey like a little feathered wildcat.

344

If the bluebird is the sapphire of the air, there is no jewel at all to compare with the glowing orange of the Baltimore oriole. He is a cousin of the blackbird, as you might know from his velvet-black wings and tail, and his flute-like whistle. His olive-backed, lemon-breasted mate sings, too, a lovely alto to his clear soprano. They sing the dearest duet you ever could hear. The orchard oriole has a black coat and hat, too, but his vest is a reddish brown, and his wings and tail are barred with white. He and his dull, olive and yellow mate sing duets, too, in richer, less whistling voices than the Baltimore. If you are not sure of the orchard orioles look for their pretty, sky-blue shoes and stockings.

No blackbird is shy, you may be sure. The orioles always fly about in plain sight, and talk freely of themselves and their affairs. A hot-headed, blustering little fellow is the oriole, noisy, restless, talkative, always whistling gaily like a happy schoolboy, in sun, wind and rain. He has scolding notes for meddlesome neighbors, too. The orchard oriole is a good policeman. When he sounds his harsh, alarm note: "Chack!" every bird in the neighborhood knows it is time to skurry to cover.

If the doctor hadn't had a cow, and a pasture lot for her with a pond in it, and low elder and hazel and briar bushes around it, he wouldn't have had some of the blackbirds nesting near him. A hedge of thorny, ruddy-flowered japonica was between the garden and the pasture. Often a gay flash of black and white, with a yellow patch on the back of the neck, tumbled up out of the meadow onto that hedge. It was the bobolink. He sang and swung and flirted his wings and tail. He chattered and gossiped and whistled. He just bubbled over with high spirits and innocent fun. Up and down the scale he sang, like a musical acrobat on a trapeze. But most of the time he just bubbled out his own saucy name.

"Bob-o-link! Bob-o-link! Spink, spank, spink!" Dear little rascal. He had no trouble at all in winning a wife!

In the cattails and rushes about the pond was always

BROWN THRASHER

a colony of red-winged blackbirds. Glossy fellows the males were, in jetty coats with red, gold-bordered shoulder knots. They strutted and danced and jumped and whistled "Bob-o-lee!" or, as some bird lovers understand: "Con-quer-ee!"

But oh, the meadow larks that nested in that pasture! This little brown-backed, and spotted-yellow-breasted singer, with the necklace of jet and white-tipped tail, is the Jenny Lind of our grasslands. You cannot walk along the edge of a clover field but he may spring up at your feet, perch on a fence or bush, and pour out a melody like flutes and violins, and human voices in vesper hymns. Yet, so few notice the meadow lark that Audubon, our greatest bird student, called him *neglecta*.

He is not a lark at all, as is the English skylark. He is a cousin of the blackbirds, the orioles and bobolinks. He walks like the black birds. He comes to us in April and sings all summer long, on the ground, on perches and on the wing. He is one of the very greatest of bird singers, rivalled only by the nightingale, the mocking bird, and the brown and hermit thrushes.

There was rivalry among the children as to who should first spy the tanager in the doctor's garden. A flash of scarlet flame across an open space, and the tanager is gone! This glowing coal of a bird with black velvet wings and tail, really belongs to a tropical family. He seems as strange among our wild birds as an orchid in a meadow. He flits about in silent places, singing a lovely little chant, as sad as the dove's but of varied melody. To his mate he sings a low sweet warble. He calls like a robin, and he "throws" his voice like a ven-tril-o-quist, so you will often think him somewhere else.

The cinnamon-brown, spotted, breasted hermit thrush of our northern pine woods can "throw" his voice, too. He is as shy as the tanager. Perhaps both of them do that to deceive hawks and squirrels and other enemies as to their whereabouts. The tanager's mate is a dull olive and yellow. Very soon he, too, takes off his scarlet and black cloak, that attracts far too much attention, and

GOLDEN PLOVER

TREE SWALLOW

wears her shabby working dress. So, if you see the tanager in his dress of flame and soot at all, it must be in the spring or early summer.

"Tweet, tweet, twitter, twitter, tweet!" Haven't you heard that often from roadside weeds, where dandelions and thistles have gone to seed? No, it isn't the speckled song sparrow of the low bushes. It is a little black and yellow cousin of his — the gold-finch, or wild canary. Canary yellow with black wings and tail, he flies as a little canoe rides the water. Such a playful, sweet-tempered, "tweet, twittering" little fellow he is. He seems to waste half the summer idling, but he is really waiting for those downy weed seeds to line his pretty nest and to feed his babies.

The finest singers of America are thrushes, blackbirds and finches. The finches all have the canary twittering songs; the blackbirds the whistling, bubbling notes. The songs of the thrushes are pure rich melody, and many of them mock the songs of the warblers, the finches and the blackbirds. Another twittering finch is the snow-white and dead-black, short-billed grosbeak, with the patches of lovely rose color on the breast and under the wings. The cardinal grosbeak, or Virginia nightingale, is a finch, too. His voice is so fine that this ruby-coated and crested singer is often caged, as is his cousin the canary.

The eaves of the doctor's barn was a great place for swallows. A big colony of them skimmed and wheeled about, the sun glistening on their blue-black forked wings and tails. They chattered, scolded intruders, and sang sweet gossipy songs to each other. They have long wings because they must fly very swiftly to catch insects. Their legs are weak because they do not use them much. The barn swallow is steel-blue on top, and reddish-brown underneath. He is the only swallow with a deep-forked "swallow tail." The purple martin is also a swallow. Mr. Martin is shiny blue-black all over; Mrs. Martin is dull brown. They like to nest in colonies, and enjoyed living in the doctor's many-roomed birdhouse. The wrens came right up to the house

CROW

and sang from the roof, the low bushes and the ground. Bill up, perky tail jerking about, this merry singer is a nervous little scold at times. "Five inches of brown fury in feathers," the doctor called Mrs. Jennie Wren. She scolded the house cat, she scolded big police-dog, Rob Roy, who was really guarding her family. She scolded every human body about the place. She even scolded that bird-bully, Mr. Blue Jay. He didn't get to come near *her* eggs! Plucky little Mother Wren! She is the gritty little terrier of the bird world!

Only the blue jay can rival the wren as a scold. A handsome fellow he is, in six shades of blue, black, white and dove color. He has a crested head, stout bill, excited wings, a terrible squalling voice and stamping feet. He is always ready for a scrap. He is a good deal of a blusterer, and one pair of blue jays is quite enough for the peace of a small garden. He'll tell you who he is as soon as he comes, by squalling his name: "Jay, Jay, Jay!"

The kingbird is as trim as you please in a coat of iron-gray, a pearl bib and an orange-red patch on his head. He cries: "Ky-rie, Kyky, ki-yi," much like a very small yelping dog. He is a cousin of the phoebe and wood-pewee, belonging to the fly-catcher family. Old red-head, the dark-blue, black and white wood pecker, with the red hood, just chuckles and drums. His cousin, the flicker, or golden-wing or yellow hammer, laughs and chatters and drums, and plays tag around tree trunks. You can always know the woodpeckers by their drumming, the big black crows by their cawing, the scary-eyed owls by their who-who-ing, the doves by their mourning, the cuckoos and the jays by their calling their own names.

Among the noisy orchard orioles in the apple trees, the brown-and-fawn colored cedar birds are apt to pass unnoticed. You may know them by the brown crest on the head, the black spectacles around the eyes, and the row of red, wax-like spots across the wing tips. They are also called cherry birds and waxwings. They have no song, only a call note, and soft, polite,

348

talking tones. They dress each other's coats with the sweetest little bows and lisping apologies, as much as to say: "Pardon me, but there's a feather out of place."

Cowbirds belong to the blackbird family, and the male is our only blackbird with a brown head. His mate is brownish-gray. She lays her eggs in the nests of other birds and lets the other birds rear her fledglings. She is not a good mother. This is very unusual, for most birds take very good care of their babies.

Starlings are blackbird-like walking birds, with purple-black upper plumage and gray speckles on head and body. They like to live in fields and orchards in summer, and in winter they gather in large flocks in cities and towns.

The yellow-bellied sapsucker belongs to the woodpecker family. Mr. Sapsucker has a red cap and throat, with long white patches on his black wings. He clings to tree trunks.

The belted kingfisher is over a foot long, with a bristling gray-blue crest on his head, and a gray-blue back. Across his white breast runs a wide blue belt. He sits motionless in a tree along a river or lake until his sharp eyes see a fish. Then he dives into the water and catches his dinner.

The ruby-throated humming bird is our smallest bird. Humming birds spend the winter in the tropics of Central and South America, and fly all the way to Canada in the summer. They are the only birds that can fly backwards. They hover over flowers, their wings moving so fast you can only see a blur. They dip their long bills in flowers to drink the nectar. They make tiny, mouse-like squeeks.

Sparrows have short, stout, cone-shaped bills so they may eat seeds easily. The indigo bunting and the goldfinch or wild canary belongs to the sparrow family. The chipping sparrows, about six inches long, can be known by their red-brown cap, gray breast, white line over the eye and black line through the eye. They are lively and cheerful as they sing their chipping song. They like to live around orchards and houses. The male indigo bunting is indigo blue all over. His mate is brown with under parts streaked, and she wags her tail sideways.

There are ever so many birds in our gardens, woods and fields. The small birds are our best singers. How many of them do you know?

# Bird Nests and Babies

One spring the doctor got all ready to put a new roof on the kitchen wing of the house. Mrs. Doctor said it leaked *ter*-ri-bly every time it rained. The carpenter came one Monday, early in April. But on the Saturday before, Mr. and Mrs. Jennie Wren had moved in under a broken shingle. They flew at that man. They told him just what they thought of him for trying to break up their housekeeping. The doctor laughed and told the man to go away, and not to come back until the wren babies were out of the nest.

A hat full of trash was taken out of that hole! There were twigs, grass, leaves, strings, rags and shavings, all laid loosely in a cup, and lined with feathers from the chicken yard. The wrens are fond of building, and any sort of a hole suits them. They will use an old shoe or a tin can. This pair built a second nest in the pocket of an old coat the doctor had hung up in a shed. If you nail some tin cans or cigar boxes up any where near the house, for nests, you can always have wrens living near you. In a wren's nest are laid as many as six flesh-colored eggs, spotted with tawny pink.

Of all the birds in the garden, the orioles made the finest nests, putting into them days of skilled labor. Orioles are weavers. The Baltimore oriole weaves a hanging purse of a nest, on the highest limb and the farthest twig of an elm tree. Sober little olive-and-yellow Mother Oriole is the artist. Gay orange-and-black Daddy Oriole is merely the hod carrier. He gathers long blades of dry grass, strands of bark from grape vines and milkweed, strings, wool, hair, thread and feathers. He has to find all these things, one at a time, and carry them up to the limb that may be fifty feet in the air. Then he sits near his little mate and sings to her. He tells her how much he loves her, and how clever she is. He brags that no squirrel can run out to that nest, or cowbird lay an egg in it, or hawk get to the bottom of it. She works quietly and steadily, and sings her pretty alto with him, sweetly.

First she takes the longest, strongest bits and ties both ends to the twig. She ties hard knots, using her bill to pull the ends through tightly. She does this until she has a number of loops, as deep as she wants the nest, for the warp, or up-and-down threads. Then she begins to weave in and out, taking a thread in her bill

SCARLET TANAGER

ROBIN

# Birds' Nests and Eggs in Trees

351

BLUE JAY

RUBY-THROATED HUMMINGBIRD

CHESTNUT-SIDED WARBLER

ROSE-BREASTED GROSBEAK

BLUEBIRD

Photos by Mrs. L. W. Brownell

CATBIRD

YELLOW-BILLED CUCKOO

# Some More Birds' Nests and Eggs

352

WHITE-EYED VIREO

ORCHARD ORIOLE

RED-WINGED BLACKBIRD

BOBWHITE

Photos, Mrs. L. W. Brownell

BALTIMORE ORIOLE

National Audubon Society

While Mrs. Oriole makes the nest, she sometimes clings upside down on it, like a circus performer. While she works, Mr. Oriole perches near by as a guard and warns other birds to stay away. He whistles and sings. Mrs. Oriole enjoys working in time to his quick, lively tune. The nest is so deep that she cannot be seen when she sits on the eggs. A father Oriole was once seen perched over the nest during the hottest part of a warm day. He really was making a bit of shade for Mrs. Oriole in the nest.

THESE EGRETS ARE NESTING ABOUT FORTY FEET HIGH

A YOUNG PELICAN'S FIRST ATTEMPTS AT FISHING

354

and poking it and pulling it back and forth. She weaves a lining of hairs and feathers. Finally she *over-casts* the top, to make it strong. When it is done she lays from five to six white eggs, blotched with splashes of brown. Then she drops to the bottom of the pocket cradle that swings in every breeze, and sits there for fourteen days.

Oh how her mate sings to her! He flashes about the tree, chasing away other birds. He relieves her when she wants a lunch. He brags and trills; he tumbles about and very nearly goes crazy with joy and pride. But one morning he is suddenly as silent as the tanager. His coat begins to fade. There are babies to be fed! Both parents must work hard, and keep quiet, to feed and protect those infants.

If you find a basket-shaped nest as skilfully woven as this, but lower down in an apple tree, it belongs to the orchard oriole. The oriole's cousin, the meadow lark, makes a more loosely woven nest on the ground, in the high grass along the edge of a meadow. Above it she ties the tall stems of grass and clover together. This makes a dome to hide the nest and to shed rain. And she makes a cunning arched passage to the nest, with the opening some distance away. The whole looks, from above, to be just a tangle of tall growth. The meadow lark is very clever, as are all the blackbirds.

The redwinged blackbird makes a loose but stout nest, braced up in a cluster of cattails or flags, or in tough wire-grass near the ground. The eggs are bluish-white with violet and brown streaks and black spots. The bobolink, rollicking fellow, is very careful to hide his shallow, shaggy nest of leaves and grass in high growths on the ground. The bobolink's eggs are stone gray, marked like the eggs of the redwing.

You cannot tell the kind of bird by the nest or its situation, any more than you can by the color of the bird. Here is one blackbird weaving a beautiful pocket high in the air, and other blackbirds nesting in loose bowls on and near the ground. Among the thrushes the robin is the best nest-builder. The bluebird uses a hole like the wren, but in an orchard tree or a fence post. The robins make a stout nest of twigs, plastered with mud and lined with soft grass, moss and feathers.

You should never tear down an old robin's nest. This is why. A pair of robins will come back to the same nest year after year. They will clean the old nest and repair it with new twigs. Mother

Robin will put on a new coat of mud, using her pretty breast for a trowel. Then she will go to some pool, take a bath, make herself tidy after her dirty work, and lay four or five eggs of robin's egg blue.

Bluebirds will use the same hole in an apple or maple tree, or a fence post, year after year, if they find it vacant. Or they will use a woodpecker's hole, or a clever bark cylinder of a nest if you put one up. Bluebirds are not builders. They put a scanty lining of weeds, grass or feathers in the best hole they can find, and Mother Bluebird lays from four to six eggs a little paler than the robin's. The mockingbird that came into the doctor's garden built a loose, round nest of crooked twigs lined with grass, rags, strings and moss, in a branch of a pine tree, only ten feet from the ground. Its eggs were a pale green, delicately spotted.

Most of the other thrushes—the brown and hermit thrush and the catbird, nest on or near the ground. The nests are clumsily made of roots, bark, sticks and leaves, rags and paper. The eggs of the brown thrush or thrasher, are cream colored, speckled with brown, like the daddy's own pretty breast. The catbird's eggs are a beautiful blue-green. You may easily mistake the nests of the brown thrush and the songsparrow. Both build on the ground, under low bushes, and of rough materials. But the song-sparrow's nest is more thickly lined with soft hair and feathers.

You wouldn't expect as wild and silent a bird as the scarlet tanager, to build a nest ten feet from the ground, at the end of the limb of a wild crabapple tree, would you? It is made of twigs, roots and shredded bark, loosely woven and lined with soft fibres. The eggs are a dull white or greenish blue, spotted with brown and violet, something like a blackbird's but more thickly spotted on the blunt ends.

The warblers are small, active birds, dressed chiefly in olive-green and yellow. The American ovenbirds and American red-starts belong to this family. Both like to live in dense woods. The male redstart has two spots of red on his wings, and a red tail tipped with black. The ovenbirds spend much time off the ground. They chatter "teacher, teacher" over and over. Oven-birds build large nests of roots and grasses on the ground. They cover the nests on top, and enter them from the side, so the nests look like ovens.

The kingbird, too, builds a big, clumsy nest in an orchard tree

## Great Horned Owl

The tufts of feathers on this owl's head look like horns. After dark, the Great Horned Owl eats many small insects and animals that otherwise would do much harm to field crops. This owl sometimes kills chickens, ducks, and geese. Owls catch their prey with their small, strong, hooked beaks. They swallow their food whole. The call of the Great Horned Owl is a deep, strong hoot, repeated five to seven times.

357

## Snowy Owl

An owl cannot roll its eyes; to see to the right, or left, it must turn its head to face that direction. Many owls do not see so well in daylight as at night. The Snowy Owl is different. It sees well in the daytime. It often hunts food while owls of other kinds are sleeping. It flies swiftly. The Snowy Owl lives in the cold regions of North America. In winter when food becomes scarce, it may travel as far south as New York. The feathers of some of these owls are almost entirely white.

VALLEY QUAIL (ABOVE) AND MOUNTAIN QUAIL (BELOW)

Valley quail and Mountain quail are found in the western and the southwestern parts of the United States. The kind of quail that inhabits the eastern part of this country is commonly known as Bobwhite. He was named for his call or song.

Bobwhite's feathers are so mottled with black, brown, gray and white that this bird is not easily seen. Bobwhite does not have a feathered crest or plume as do the Valley and the Mountain quail.

Quail are game birds; their meat has such excellent flavor that sportsmen hunt them for food. Most states have laws that protect these birds from hunters, especially during the nesting season. They should be protected; they are cheerful and friendly, but they are also useful. They eat beetles that destroy potato and cucumber vines. They feed on boll weevils and worms that harm corn, clover and cotton fields. In addition, they eat many undesirable weed seeds.

or maple, right out in plain sight. But he is ready to defend it with much bustle and talk, telling everyone that this is his castle and no visitors are welcome. The jaybird builds a loose nest, too, but in a high branch. And he doesn't disdain to use the deserted nest of a crow. That shows his good sense, for the crow flies high and makes a stout nest of sticks and all sorts of things. He stuffs all the cracks with moss, and he plasters it outside with mud so it is often good for a couple of seasons. Besides, he lines it thickly with horse hair, moss and wool, for little crow babies are perfectly naked.

The swallows are even better masons than the robins and crows. They make their entire nests of little pills of mud, mixed with straw and their own saliva. Like the robins, too, they repair their old nests. A barn swallow colony comes back to the old home and looks over the old battered rows of mud and straw nests under the eaves and along the rafters.

Little phoebe with her "pewit-pewee" is confiding, too, like the wrens. She builds her nest of moss and mud around dwelling houses, and under low bridge arches. The cedarbird likes a cherry or a cedar tree. She makes a large nest of clover stems, pine needles, grass and shredded bark. She is a late builder although she comes early. It is June or July before she lays her four or five clay-colored eggs. The goldfinch doesn't build until there are the softest thistle and dandelion seeds to line her pretty nest of fine grasses. She builds it in the crotch of a tree, not over twenty feet high, and in it lays from four to six pretty bluish-white eggs.

If the orioles are weavers and the swallows masons, the woodpeckers are carpenters. A pair, working together, chisel out a home in hard, clean wood. Old red-head's nest is often a foot deep. The door to it is a round auger hole that goes into the tree, then curves downward and swells out. The hole is the shape of a crooknecked gourd. Father Red-head chisels for twenty minutes, then the mother relieves him. Both of them work, in relays, from dawn until nightfall. Flat-chested, hump-shouldered, stout toilers, the woodpeckers have to dig their clean nests, and then dig for grubs to feed themselves and babies. They are the hard laborers of the bird-world.

What a hurried, worried time it is for the parent birds when the baby birds are out of their shells. The nests must be cleaned

YELLOW-BILLED CUCKOO

of the eggshells and dirt, and every baby kept perfectly clean. Crow babies are naked and very tender skinned. Bird babies look to be all mouths. They lie helplessly in the nest, bills wide open, crying every few minutes for food, and what a lot of it they can eat!

Every few minutes one or the other of the robin parents hurries to the nest with a mouthful of worms. The babies just lie there, big yellow bills open, and eat two or three times their own weight of worms every day. From dawn until dark a worm must be found every two minutes to keep a nest full of young robins fed. That means several hundred in a day for one brood!

The bluebirds forage the lawns and orchards for grubs and insects, the blackbird the corn-field for cut worms; the orioles for small caterpillars; the woodpeckers for wood borers; the swallows for winged fliers. Nothing that bores, or creeps, or flies, or burrows in the ground, but goes to feed the nestling. Wild and tame fruits and weed seeds are hunted, too.

When they come out of the nests every kind of bird baby acts differently. The orioles are cry-babies, crying to be fed even when they are able to fly. The wren babies make for the nearest holes—a water spout or rat hole, perhaps—and have to be coaxed and scolded to safe perches in bushes. Little speckle-breasted robin babies hop after their parents and soon learn to be quiet. The woodpecker babies are stupid and clumsy, and expect to be fed a long time. The jays are scarcely out of the nest before they begin to scold. The kingbirds are the most sensible of all. They mind their parents, stick close together, and learn how to look out for themselves.

When the bird babies are out you can see several of the prettiest things in bird family life. The older birds are feeding the young ones, on the wing. And you can see many a lesson given in singing, in food-finding, and in skurrying out of sight when alarm notes are sounded. You can watch the little ones being taught to bathe in tiny pools, or to flutter in the dust bath.

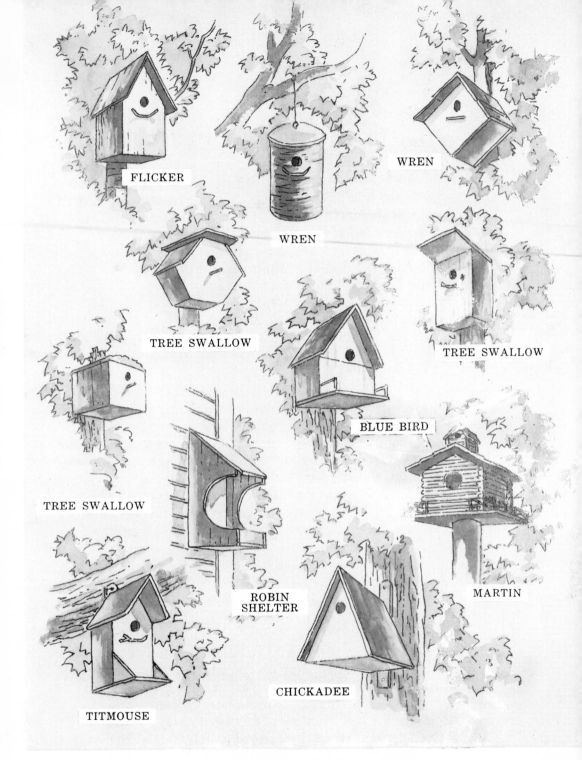

FLICKER

WREN

WREN

TREE SWALLOW

TREE SWALLOW

TREE SWALLOW

BLUE BIRD

MARTIN

ROBIN SHELTER

CHICKADEE

TITMOUSE

# Nesting Places for Birds

Good nesting places attract birds. Some birds prefer one kind of nesting place while others choose an entirely different kind.

# Little Friends in Feathers

One sunny Saturday afternoon in June, a tanned, dusty-legged boy came to the doctor's side porch. In one hand he had a soft, limp bundle of snow-white, dead-black and rose-colored feathers. In the other he carried a sling-shot. A shame-faced lad he was, for not a boy in the town would purposely kill one of the doctor's birds. He had just aimed at the tempting singer on the picket fence of the vegetable garden.

"But doctor," he said, "perhaps you don't know that this bird was eating your green peas. I saw him."

"Let us see," said the doctor. He opened the little crop, under the rosy spot on the breast that would throb with song no more. Yes, there were as many as two pods full of young peas. But the little vestibule to the stomach was packed full of potato bugs—the striped Colorado beetles that were eating all the potato patches in the town.

Out of the picket fence the mother grosbeak had all her babies in a row, and was feeding them the beetles. Black-headed grosbeaks were there, too. In a few days the doctor's potato plants were picked clean, and the birds were foraging in nearby gardens. "One pair of grosbeaks brings up a brood of four or five in a season," said the doctor. "One pair of Colorado beetles breeds to 50,000,000. For the good potatoes these pretty singers help me grow, I can spare them a whole row of peas."

That was a lesson one little boy never forgot. The doctor always opened the crops and stomachs of dead birds. In a robin's stomach in June he found a few orchard cherries, among the insects and wild fruits.

"The robin comes to us in March," he explained to a sober little group. "For three months he has nothing but worms, ground beetles and dry, winter berries to eat. He brings up one brood of babies on such food. No wonder he wants a few juicy cherries in June. Nine-tenths of the robin's food is insects and wild fruits. Only in June and July does he eat cherries to pay for the six months' work he does for us so cheerfully. He eats beetles, grubs, worms, caterpillars, spiders, snails, grasshoppers, wild grapes, blue-berries, service berries, choke berries, black

CHESTNUT-BACKED CHICKADEE

alder and holly-berries, rose hips and the seeds of sumac.

There were always dead birds for the doctor to study. Woeful little tragedies happened in the nests. Once, a pretty mother oriole was hanged by a loop of horse hair, in a nest she was weaving. For hours the mate made wild lament for his loss. Then, a high wind tumbled the half-finished nest and the dead weaver to the ground. Nothing but insects were in the little stomach — beetles, ants, wasps, spiders, bark scales, plant lice and caterpillars. In midsummer the oriole eats a few grapes and peas. Can't we spare her those for the countless insects she eats and feeds to her babies?

A barnswallow, hurt in some way on its northward flight, had fed on cotton-boll weevil, in flying over the young cotton plants in the south. And she had eaten flies, mosquitoes, gnats and little wasps, and in her stomach were the broken wings of the gadfly that stings horses. The doctor put more brackets under the eaves of the barn, on which these little friends of barnyard animals could brace their nests.

For the housewrens and bluebirds the doctor put up box nests. For the phoebes he had a grape-arbor and a vine-draped porch. For the chickadees he planted a thick hedge; for the brown thrush and song sparrow low-growing shrubs. There was a mulberry tree for the orchard birds to feed upon, a cedar tree for waxwing. And along the pasture he let the elderberry bushes, wild blackberry briars and briar roses grow, for the fruit. There were sumac bushes, too, and alder saplings, a choke cherry and other wild fruit and seed-making trees. For years and years he kept on telling his neighbors that nearly all of our wild birds are insect, wild fruit and weed seed eaters.

Each kind of bird has its special work to do. Woodpeckers go under the bark of forest trees for wood-boring beetles and grubs. The cuckoo, or raincrow, eats hairy caterpillars. The only other birds that can manage these are the orioles. In the stomach of one cuckoo the doctor found two hundred webworms. The

VERMILION FLYCATCHER

robins clear our lawns; the bluebirds, catbirds and cedarbirds forage in the orchards. The wood thrushes and flickers feed on the ground in groves. The meadow larks, bobolinks and redwings hunt in the pastures and swamps. The swallows, the kingbirds, the phoebes and other flycatchers are raiders of the air. Wrens forage in low plants, shrubs, and in cracks and crannies of house walls and fences. Hawks and owls hunt mice and moles. In August, all the insect-eating birds make a feast of grasshoppers. One brood of robins eats half a million insects and larvae in a summer, and not a thousand cherries.

For many, many years scattered bird lovers told their neighbors these things. Some of them were laughed at, some only half believed. The wild birds became fewer and fewer. The nests were robbed, the singers killed for their pretty wings. The farmers drove the birds away. Then we began to have wormy orchard fruits, army worms, canker and cutworms, tent caterpillars, boring weevils, flies, plagues of grasshoppers and Colorado beetles. Countless unseen enemies ate up the farm crops, orchards and gardens, and even the grass on the lawns. We looked everywhere for help except up in the air.

Then it was that our government began to study our bird friends. In the farmer's bureau in the capital at Washington, thousands of little stomachs were opened, in every month of the year. Every bit of food found in them was written down. We know, now, just what every wild bird eats, in every season. If a bird has a bad habit we can help him cure it. The crow pulls up young corn plants for the softened seeds. But if the seeds are soaked in tar water before planting he will not touch them. But he will go into the corn fields for cut worms.

We have taken the trouble, here, to find out for you, from many books, and from agricultural bulletins printed by our government, just what our commonest wild birds eat, and how they help us. First of all remember that:

Woodpeckers, cuckoos, swallows (swifts and martins), phoebes, pewees, kingbirds and other flycatchers, wrens, hawks, nighthawks (bull bats) and owls, live almost wholly on animal food. The chickadees are insect feeders, too. They stay with us all winter, and hunt out sleeping flies, and the eggs and chrysalises of moths and beetles. The kingbird is called the bee martin, and has been accused of eating honey bees. It has been found that it eats only drone bees. Drones have white faces, and no stingers. And it catches the robber-fly that destroys bees. Kingbirds protect poultry yards and other song birds by driving away hawks, crows and jaybirds. They eat such wild fruits as elder berries. Hawks and owls live mostly on mice, moles and other small rodents. Woodpeckers eat the fruits of the dogwood, Virginia creeper, poison ivy, sumac and the nuts of beech trees. No farm, garden, orchard, park or lawn can afford to be without the insect feeders. A woodpecker or kingbird should never be disturbed. Wrens, swallows, phoebes and chickadees should be encouraged to nest near our homes.

Among the useful seed eaters are doves, pigeons, and native sparrows, and the goldfinches or wild canaries. Mourning doves eat the seeds of weeds and the gleanings of grain fields. One third of the food of our native sparrows in summer is insects, but the hard seeds of grasses, weeds and waste grain is the chief food. The goldfinch eats weed and thistle seeds, and bush buds. A very useful bird on a farm is the quail (bobwhite or partridge). Two thirds of its food is weed seeds, the rest harmful insects and waste grain. The English sparrow is a pest. He lives in flocks, is quarrelsome, drives away our song birds, and eats only the useful grains. He should be treated as a pest.

All the rest of our wild birds use a mixed diet of insects, seeds and fruits. The amounts differ with each, and with the same birds in different seasons. Thus, from March to June, the robin lives on ground beetles, larvae, angle worms, spiders, snails and dry berries left over winter on bushes. He helps himself to orchard cherries in June.

SPARROW HAWK

MOURNING DOVE

Late cherries he does not touch, for then the choke cherries, elder berries, cranberries, briar berries and sumac seeds are ripe. The Russian mulberry, that ripens with the early cherries, he really prefers. Plant a mulberry tree, and fruit-bearing shrubs and vines on the edge of an orchard, and the robin, bluebird, catbird, cedarbird, jays and many other birds will do little harm to the cultivated fruits. In August, the robins eat grasshoppers and wild fruits.

Three fourths of the bluebird's food is insects, the rest wild fruits and seeds. The meadow lark's food is three fourths ground insects, the rest waste grain and weed seeds. Orioles live almost entirely on insects, hairy caterpillars forming one third of the food. They eat a little fruit in mid-summer. All the grosbeaks are enemies of the Colorado beetle. One family of grosbeaks can keep a good-sized patch of potatoes free of this pest. They also eat the pupa of the codling moth that lays the apple worm.

The grosbeaks eat some green peas, small fruits and waste grain. They pay ten thousand times over for every useful thing they eat. Cedar (cherry or waxwing) birds, like the robins, eat some early cherries. But they prefer mulberries or cedar berries. In late summer and fall they live mostly on weed seeds and wild fruits. The nestlings, at first, are fed on insects. These birds eat the elm-leaf beetle and plant lice as well as grasshoppers. The catbird eats about half animal and half vegetable food. Insects and wild fruits and seeds form the bulk of its food. A government report says of it: "The catbird has a bad name, but it does more good than harm." The mocking bird, brown thrasher and nearly all the thrushes have much the same food habits as the robin and bluebird. Two thirds of their food is insects, the rest wild and tame fruits.

Jays eat everything: seeds, acorns, nuts, fruits, insects, the eggs and young of other birds. They eat mice, fish, snails, and they rob orchards.

366

With the blackbirds it is a different story. Orioles and mead-owlarks are among our most useful bird friends. The redwings' food is eighty-five per cent insects and weed seeds, eaten in marshes where many weeds and crop enemies breed. Less than ten per cent of its food is grain. The crow blackbird eats forty per cent of grain. The bobolink feeds on insects and weed seeds when nesting in the north, but rice when migrating.

American or bald eagles have a wing spread of seven feet. They are dark brown, with snow-white head and neck. Their principal food is fish, so they live near water. They build their great nests of branches high up on cliffs or in tall trees, and re-turn to them year after year, each year building the nest larger until it may weigh a ton.

Water birds are of three kinds. There are the kingfishers, who fly down from trees into the water and catch fish in their bills. There are the long-legged, long-toed waders, with long necks and bills, like the cranes, who walk in the water and dip their necks down to get fish. And there are the swimmers, like the swans and geese and ducks, with long necks and wide bills for digging in the muddy bottoms of ponds, where they find food.

The crow does pull up corn and rob song bird's nests. To the credit of the crow are the field and barn mice, moles, May beetles, June bugs, cutworms and grasshoppers he eats and feeds to his family. The crow eats no orchard fruit, and only a little corn in the milk.

Birds are our little brothers of the air who help us keep the earth green and fruitful. They alone are able to keep the unseen armies of insect enemies in check. We need their help.

They have so many human ways. They love their mates; they care so tenderly for their babies. They have such skill, such industry, such courage, such devotion to duty, such grace of movement and beauty of plumage and voice. Don't you think, since they help us so much, we should be willing to help them a little? All they want is protection, and a little help in the kind of food they need, where wild fruits and seeds do not grow. Pro-vide nesting places for them about town houses. Where they are wanted they will come, year after year. Then, when they fly away in the autumn, we will know that they have helped us grow grains and fruits, vegetables, shade trees and flowers.

## MALLARDS

Probably the most widely distributed of all the wild ducks. They are to be found in Europe, Asia, and Africa as well as North America. They are closely related to our domestic white ducks, and with protection will probably not become dangerously reduced in numbers.

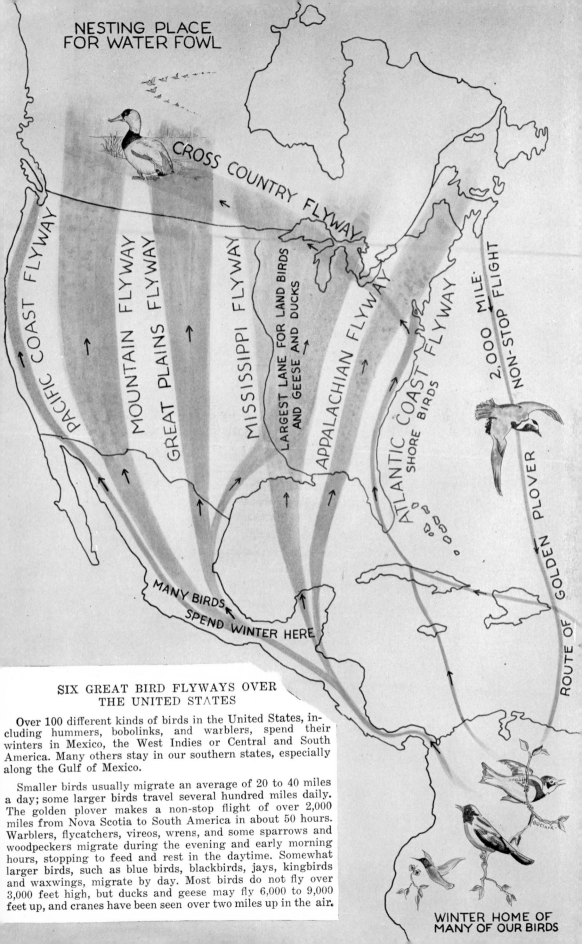

NESTING PLACE
FOR WATER FOWL

CROSS COUNTRY FLYWAY

PACIFIC COAST FLYWAY

MOUNTAIN FLYWAY

GREAT PLAINS FLYWAY

MISSISSIPPI FLYWAY

LARGEST LANE FOR LAND BIRDS AND GEESE AND DUCKS

APPALACHIAN FLYWAY

ATLANTIC COAST FLYWAY
SHORE BIRDS

2,000 MILE NON-STOP FLIGHT

ROUTE OF GOLDEN PLOVER

MANY BIRDS
SPEND WINTER HERE

## SIX GREAT BIRD FLYWAYS OVER THE UNITED STATES

**Over 100** different kinds of birds in the United States, including hummers, bobolinks, and warblers, spend their winters in Mexico, the West Indies or Central and South America. Many others stay in our southern states, especially along the Gulf of Mexico.

Smaller birds usually migrate an average of 20 to 40 miles a day; some larger birds travel several hundred miles daily. The golden plover makes a non-stop flight of over 2,000 miles from Nova Scotia to South America in about 50 hours. Warblers, flycatchers, vireos, wrens, and some sparrows and woodpeckers migrate during the evening and early morning hours, stopping to feed and rest in the daytime. Somewhat larger birds, such as blue birds, blackbirds, jays, kingbirds and waxwings, migrate by day. Most birds do not fly over 3,000 feet high, but ducks and geese may fly 6,000 to 9,000 feet up, and cranes have been seen over two miles up in the air.

WINTER HOME OF
MANY OF OUR BIRDS

# BIRD TOOLS FOR SECURING THEIR FOOD

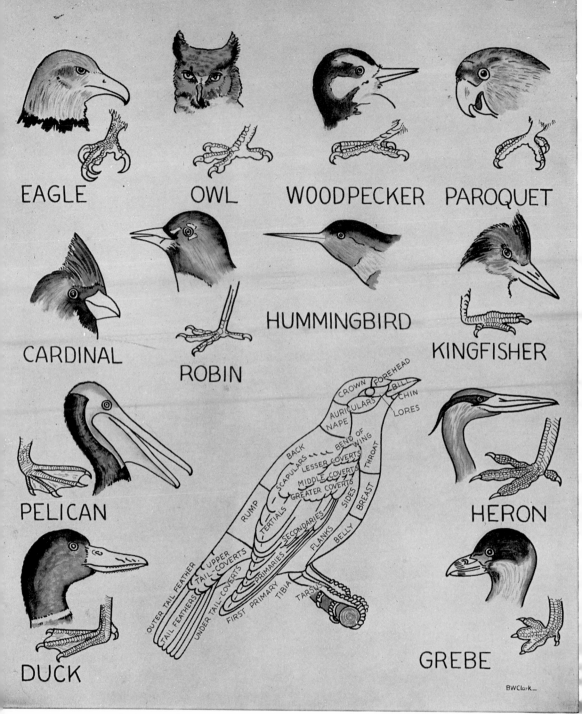

EAGLE  OWL  WOODPECKER  PAROQUET

CARDINAL  HUMMINGBIRD  KINGFISHER

ROBIN

PELICAN  HERON

DUCK  GREBE

BWClark

Eagles and owls use their beaks to tear flesh and their talons to seize mice and other small animals. Woodpeckers peck holes in trees to find grubs and insects; they cling to tree trunks with their toes. Paroquets pick and crack seeds with their beaks, often perching on a limb and holding food in the claws of one foot. Cardinals eat seeds, humming birds suck nectar from flowers, and robins use their bills to peck and pull worms from the ground; all three are perchers. Kingfishers sit on limbs watching for fish and dive to capture their prey. The swimming pelicans dive for fish, which they put in a pouch hanging from the lower bill. Herons use their long, thin legs for wading and their long bills for catching fish, frogs, and other water animals. Ducks dig their wide bills in the mud for water animals and roots; grebes catch fish; both use their webbed feet for swimming.

PHOTOS AT TOP BY GEOFFREY LANDESMAN

Most bears love honey as much as children do, and they can walk on two feet like a man. The big Alaskan brown bear taking a drink is the largest kind of bear in the world. When winter comes, mother polar bear lets the snow cover her and goes to sleep for many weeks. Her warm breath melts a hole in the snow for fresh air. Toward spring her babies are born. You see her washing the creamy white fur of her yawning cub.

# The Story of Wild Animals You Would Like to Know

Wild animals have a wonderful fascination for children. About the traits, habits and homes of those most commonly to be seen in menageries and city park zoos, they never tire of hearing. Ample accounts of these animals, giving the classifications and main facts by which they may be identified, are to be found under the appropriate headings in the body of this work. Those accounts should always be read first. The pictures should be studied, and drawings and clay models of the animals made. In no other way than by the graphic arts, can the facts of life be so firmly and accurately impressed on a child's mind. The child is then ready for peeps into the wonderland of the life of wild creatures. Unconsciously, and with the keenest interest, he absorbs a great deal of geography, zoology and related subjects, and sees the animals in their relation to human beings, their place in literature and folklore, and their claim on his sympathy.

## Big Brother Bear

W'y, wunst they wuz a Little Boy went out
In the woods, to shoot a Bear—an' he
Wuz goin' along—an' goin' along, you know,
An' purty soon he heerd somefin go *"Wooh!"*—
'ist that-a-way—*"Woo-ooh!"*—*James Whitcomb Riley.*

You ought to get Mr. Riley's poems and read the bear story that little Alex, who couldn't talk plain, but who knew all about bears, " 'ist maked up his-own-se'f."

Did you ever think why little American boys and girls know more stories about bears, and are more interested in bears than they are in any other wild animals? It must be because white children and bears are such old acquaintances. They have always lived near neighbors, both in the old world and in the new. In northern countries, where white people live, there never have been any lions or other big, flesh-eating beasts, so Mr. Bear has had the woods and

2—6

mountains and frozen oceans very much to himself. Besides, although he can kill deer and buffalo bigger than himself, he rarely attacks men unless they hunt him. If caught as a cub, he can be tamed and taught all sorts of cunning tricks. And he is so bright and does so many almost human things, that we rather like him, even if we are afraid of him.

Little Alex knew that "bears kin climb up higher in the trees than any little boys in all the wo-r-r-ld!" that the big father and mother bears "*get mad*" if you bother their babies; that they think out new ways to escape traps and catch their enemies. So now, maybe this story is really true:

"Once upon a time, a Puritan boy who came to live in America was lost in the forest. He climbed a tall tree to look over the country to find himself. The tree was hollow to the bottom. Suddenly he slipped and fell into the well-like hole, and dropped plump onto something soft and warm and squirmy and grunty. He knew at once he had fallen into a bear's den onto the cubs, and was badly scared; for he couldn't climb out. 'Way, 'way up he could see a round patch of blue sky. Then he couldn't see it. The hole was corked like a bottle by mother bear coming home. He remembered that a bear always comes down backwards, just as a boy does.

"Down she scrambled, scratching and 'woof-ing,' and backed her hairy body right into the boy. He grabbed her shaggy coat and hung on for dear life, and screamed. Very likely the bear thought a wild cat was on her back. Wild cats have terrible claws, and the bear was where she couldn't fight. So she climbed up as fast as she could, and pulled the boy out of the hole. They both 'ran fourteen miles in fifteen days and never looked behind them'."

That must have been one of the smaller black bears that used to be so common everywhere in American woods. The black bear is so bright that the Indians called him "brother." They never killed one purposely. The little Puritan boy was right in thinking that she would come down backwards as did the brown bear in the woods of England. Both of these land bears do many things like boys. They can stand up on their hind legs and "box" with the fore paws, as if they were trained in a school gymnasium. They can walk on the hind legs and carry a cub or a squealing pig in their arms, as your mother carries the baby. They eat meat only if they can get nothing better. Really they prefer blackberries, honey and nuts, just as children do. *And*—they make tracks with the entire soles of their five-toed feet, that look like bare-footed men's tracks. The Indians were sometimes fooled by these tracks of Brother Bear. To the people of Northern Europe, who wondered over these human-looking foot-prints, the brown bear was called "the wise old man in the fur cloak."

Brown bear cubs always were easily tamed. In Northern Japan a people called Ainos fatten bear cubs for food. When small they play with the children, and are not shut up until they become big and rough. They are as playful as puppies. Hundreds of years ago trained bears were led by chains about the old walled cities of Europe, and made to dance and tumble and pull carts. Very likely bears, and many other wild animals, were tamer in the days when there were fewer people and bigger forests. In Yellowstone Park, in the Rocky Mountains, where hunters are not allowed to shoot or trap them, black and cinnamon bears come right up to the hotels in the woods to eat scraps from the table.

Mr. Thompson Seton tells all about these bears, and their bright and comical ways, in his story of "Johnny Bear." Johnny was a cub that worried his mother. He was an only child, and very much spoiled and peevish. He would poke his silly head into every sort of danger. He was so greedy he often had the stomachache, and he got his paws fast in tomato cans and jam pots. So, once she had to box his ears!

We can't all go to Yellowstone Park and take snap-shot pictures of bears from the hotel verandas, but nearly all of us can see them in menageries and city park zoos. There you can see black and brown, cinnamon, "grizzly" and polar bears. They all belong to one family, as you can easily see from their clumsy bodies, shuffling walk, shaggy coats and bear-y faces. But, in many ways, they are as different from each other as white, black, brown and yellow people.

The old world brown bear is the tamest of all. He will sit upon his haunches, cross his paws over his breast and catch peanuts in his mouth. Sometimes, when the band plays, he will dance and gambol about like a big, playful dog. The smaller, fine-coated black bear is friendly sometimes; but often he climbs the oak tree in his pit, folds his limp body across a big limb, like a big bear rug, and sulks or sleeps. You couldn't coax him down with a pot of honey! The big "grizzly" bear has an ugly temper. He snarls. President Theodore Roosevelt said his real name is "Grisly," or horrid, and you believe it. He is a huge, ugly beast with long teeth and long gray hair about his head. The big white polar bear, who weighs as much as an ox, doesn't pay any attention to anybody. He just prowls and prowls in an uneasy, lonesome way about his pit, until you feel sorry for him. His thick fur and fat body make him uncomfortable, very likely. When, on a hot day, a keeper gives him a ton of ice to lie on, he seems happier. If he turns his big paws up you can see that he is rough-shod, with hairy bristles all over the soles of his feet, for traveling on ice and snow.

Suddenly, for no cause that you can see, the bears in all the pits will shuffle over to the bars, rear upon their hind legs and "woof!" They smell the keeper coming with bread. Bears do not see very well out of their small eyes, and are rather dull of hearing, but they have wonderful noses for news, especially news of food and of enemies. If the wind is right, Mr. Wild Bear can smell a hunter and his gunpowder a mile away, and he gets out of a dangerous neighborhood as fast as he can travel.

He can travel fast, too. For all he is so clumsy he can run as well as he can climb. But he is not built for jumping, or for turning easily and quickly. Old hunters know this, so when a bear chases them they sometimes escape by turning sharp corners, or by zigzaging. This puzzles a bear and wears him out. Hunters never climb big trees, for the bear can go right up after them. When they climb small trees bears have been known to put their big arms around the trunk and try to shake them down. Or they sit at the foot of the tree and wait. As little Alex says: "That bear 'ist won't go 'way, 'ist growls 'round there, an' the Little Boy he haf to stay up in the tree all night." Bears are clever about getting out of tight places, too. Here is a story about a clever bear that is told by a naturalist.

A dozen men were in the Rocky Mountains of Canada laying out a route for a new railroad when they saw a big cinnamon bear in a tree. He had gone up for honey or a squirrel's store of nuts, or just for a nap, perhaps. The men had no guns, but they had axes and crowbars, so they thought they could manage Mr. Bear. They chopped the tree nearly down, the bear lying still and watching them. When the tree began to fall he put his forepaws over his head, rolled up into a big ball and dropped. He upset some of the men and surprised the others so that he had time to scramble to his feet and run away. I shouldn't wonder if that bear were still laughing at those men.

Bears will not run from danger and leave their cubs behind. A cub can never be captured unless father and mother bear are dead, or far away from home. They hide their babies very cleverly in caves, hollow trees or under old logs where they make their winter dens. They keep the cubs hidden there for weeks and months after they are born, for bear babies are as blind as kittens, as naked as little birds, and perfectly helpless at first. They are fed with milk at their mother's breast, so she stays with the cubs while father bear goes foraging for food for her. Mother Bear is as cross—as a bear. You know that's as cross as any one can be. She will try to kill anyone who comes near her babies.

All wild animals are fond of their mates and babies, and will fight for them. But there are few that are as brave and loving as the polar bears. Explorers and whalers tell stories that make the tears come to your eyes. In that lonely waste of frozen land and water, a polar bear family seems almost human in their close affection. In the winter the mother and cubs stay in the warm cave, but the father cannot sleep all winter long as the land bears do. He must go out into the Arctic night for food. He watches seal and walrus holes as patiently as the Eskimo. He climbs icy cliffs. He is often carried out to sea on floating ice, and he swims back, miles and miles. In the summer the whole family hunt together. If one parent is killed the other will not desert the body. Neither will leave a dead or wounded cub, but will stand over it, lick the face and wound, pet it, coax it to get up, and will fight to the death rather than be driven away. They are terrible in their grief and rage.

There are three kinds of bears—land, water and honey bears. Of course all bears love honey, and will risk being stung on their tender noses to get it. But the honiest honey bear lives in the East Indies. In his Mowgli stories, Mr. Kipling has a honey bear that he calls Baloo. This animal is called the jungle bear because he sleeps in the shady jungle all day, and also the sloth, because he is so sleepy and moves about so slowly, and also the honey eater. He and the sun bear, who loves the sun as the jungle bear loves the shade, have long upper lips that look as if they had been stung by angry bees, and stretchy rubbery tongues. They can push this lip and tongue into an ant's nest and suck up a whole village with a greedy noise you can hear yards away. They eat bees and ants, ants' eggs, rice plants, fruits, honey and even flowers. In South

America are numbers of honey bears. Some of them climb cocoanut trees and drink the milk of green nuts.

These are about all the animals you know as bears, but there are several cousins of the bears who are all clever. They are famous climbers, diggers, fighters and swimmers. The raccoon or 'coon, that Southern negroes love to hunt, is the plucky little tree-bear. He is only two feet long, but he will fight a dozen dogs and sometimes get away. Here is something funny about the 'coon. He likes his food wet, or clean, or something. When he finds something to eat he takes it to a brook and washes it. In Germany the 'coon is called the washing bear. In a wild state the big bears do not seem to have this habit. But when the loaves of bread are brought to the pits in park zoos, all the bears roll it into the running water and soak it before eating it.

There is one thing bears are afraid of—guess! You never will. Mosquitoes.

Away up in Alaska where the biggest golden brown bear of all lives, and the glacier bear on the ice rivers, the summers are short and hot. There mosquitoes breed by millions on the vast swamps. The tip of a bear's nose is quite naked, moist and sensitive, like a dog's. He needs it that way for smelling. And, of course, his eyes have little protection. The mosquitoes swarm in clouds about poor Bruin and sting and sting him. He can fell a buffalo with one box of his big paw, but he cannot fight these little pests. He just turns tail and runs!

Long, long ago, the people in a far-away cold country called Finland had a beautiful story about the bear. They called him Otso. This story was put into verse like that of Hiawatha, and sung by mothers to put children to sleep:

> Otso, thou, O forest lover,
> Bear of honey-paws and fur-robes,
> Learn that Waina Moinen follows,
> That the singer comes to meet thee;
> Hide thy claws within thy mittens,
> Let thy teeth remain in darkness,
> Mighty Otso, much beloved,
> Honey-eater of the mountains.

Isn't that a pretty song of Brother Bear? Maybe that's why you like to take Teddy Bear to bed with you.

# Pet Pussy and King Lion

Men have known lions longer than they have bears. They have lived right next door to lions for thousands of years, but they never called a lion "brother." They never felt as friendly as that toward this fierce, proud beast. He has always been King of the dry plains of Africa and the hot jungle of India. In the menagerie and zoo he keeps everyone at a distance, and seems to feel very much above all the other animals, and even men. If he could understand that he has a cousin so small, so tame, and so playful that little children make a pet of him, he might just roar with rage and shame.

The lion is only a very big wild cat. Your pet kitten is like him in more ways than you imagine. In fact, pussy is a live and lively book on lions. Live books are better than printed ones, and much more interesting. Pussy walks and runs and crouches and springs exactly as a lion does. She watches a mouse hole and springs on her prey as a lion does, too. Turn her on her back and look at her paws. There are five toes on her front paws, one of them a sort of thumb, but only four toes on her hind paws. Did you know that? On each toe is a little curved toe-nail, as sharp as a little sickle. Pussy keeps her claws inside her pretty, soft fur mittens most of the time. But she can push them out as quick as a wink, pull them back again and scratch exactly like a lion. Under the toes and the balls of the feet are soft, naked cushions, so pussy makes no sound when she walks. All the wild cats—the lions, tigers and leopards, the jaguars, panthers and lynxes have feet just like the house cat's.

Now look at pussy's head. She has upright, outward-turning ears. She must hear well because she hunts at night. On each side of her mouth are long stiff hairs. These are feelers to keep her from putting her head into a smaller hole than her body can go through. Her eyes are the strangest of all. There are windows, or pupils, in them, for letting the light in, as there are in your eyes. In the dark these windows are big and round, so they shine like little yellow moons. But in the daytime, or in a lamp-lighted room, those pupils close to a narrow, up-and-down slit to keep the light out. Pussy can see in the dark so well because she can open her eye-windows so wide. Some of the lesser wild cats shut the pupils of their eyes to slits, but the lion, tiger and leopard draw their pupils up into little round holes. In that one thing the lion is more like boys and girls than pet kittens.

Put your finger in pussy's mouth. What sharp teeth she has. They pierce like the points of carpet tacks. When she licks your hand her tongue feels like a file. A lion's teeth are like daggers, and his tongue is so rough he can scrape bones clean with it. Lions lap water with their tongues, too. Pussy doesn't like to get her feet wet, and lions just hate water, except to drink. That is queer, for many of the wild cats love water. The tigers of India swim across small arms of the sea. They haunt river banks and swamps, wade in up to their necks to drink, wallow in the mud, then wash off and roll in the sand. This love of water gets them into trouble with crocodiles. The jaguar, or South American tiger, likes turtles and catches them by swimming.

All the wild cats wash their faces with their paws. Perhaps you have wondered why your big cat likes to go to a quiet, shady place and sleep a good deal in the daytime, and then prowl about and make dreadful noises at night. She learned that habit thousands of years ago when all cats were wild, and she never quite gets over it, no matter how tame she seems. She will try to hide her babies, too. On farms, where there are fine hiding places, mother cats will make a den under the barn floor, in the haymow, or in a hollow log up in the woods. If you try to follow her to find her kittens she will mislead you in the cleverest way. The mother lion carries her kittens by taking the loose skin at the back of the neck between her teeth, just as the house cat does.

The lion makes his den in a rocky cave hidden by bushes, on the edge of a wide sandy plain where many antelopes, deer, zebra and other grazing animals roam. In one thing he is better than the house cat. When he is about three or four years old, and has a short, fine silky mane, of which he is as proud as big brother is of his downy mustache, the lion picks out a mate to go to housekeeping. These two stay together just as human fathers and mothers do, all their lives, and they sometimes live to be fifty years of age. When they find a house that suits them they don't like to move. You know tame cats like places better than they do people, and often refuse to go with the most loving little mistress to a new home.

There's one thing that lions can't do that cats can. They can't climb trees. But tigers, leopards, panthers and all the other big, wild cats are great climbers, so it must be that lions have lived so long where there are few trees that they just forgot how to climb. The lion has forgotten to have stripes, or spots, too. His coat is of a uniform yellowish-brown, the color of sand and dry grass. All the other wild cats, and many tame ones, have beautiful markings. The tiger is banded in black and reddish fawn. The leopard is covered with big black polka dots on a golden fawn ground. The jaguar, or South American tiger is dot-in-a-ring spotted. But here is a curious thing. Although the grown up lion hasn't a sign of a spot or stripe about him, lion cubs often show faint markings that disappear as they grow older.

Scientists tell us that the young of many animals show, in some such way, how their ancestors looked ages and ages ago. Once, perhaps, there were no lions, as we see them today, only big striped and spotted cats that slowly changed into lions because of the open plains they had to hunt on. In the dancing sunspots and shadows of the leafy jungles, and in the foliage of thick trees, the tiger and leopard are safely hidden, but on level, treeless, brown plains they could be seen a long way off. But, while he had to paint out his spots and stripes, the African lion grew a beautiful dark mane that makes his head appear much larger, fiercer and nobler than that of any other cat. He grew a tuft of hair and a horny cone on the tip of his tail to lash himself into a rage. And he grew a terrifying roar, too!

Maybe you have heard a big African lion roar in a zoo. You can hear him a mile. That roar starts all the other animals. The tiger screams, the jaguar cries *piouw!* something like pussy's *meauw.* The bear " 'ist growls," the buffaloes bellow, the elephants trumpet. All the fierce, fighting animals are thrown into a rage by that roar, and the timid ones tremble with fear. Some of them run, but others seem unable to move.

Maybe that is why the lion roars when he is on the hunt—to paralyze his prey with fear. He lies on the bank of a stream waiting, as pussy waits at a mouse hole, for some timid antelope, whose only safety is in his heels, to come down to drink. Then he springs with a roar. The way he roars in a zoo isn't *anything* to what he can do in the roaring line at home. He has several kinds of roars. Sometimes he moans like the wind in the tree tops. Sometimes he rumbles like faraway thunder. Sometimes he gets his neighbors to help him give a desert concert on a dark, stormy night. But it is worst of all when one party of lions meets another and they all roar at

Siamese cats have cream-colored
bodies, with brown faces,
ears, paws and tails.

↑

White Persian cat.

Maltese cat is bluish-grey.

↓ Persian cats have long, silky hair.

A GROUP OF YOUNG LIONS

LIONS

382

TIGER

LEOPARD

one another for hours. You know what a dreadful noise cats can make when they quarrel on the back fence. Lions act the same way, only worse, and they can be heard miles and miles.

Ostriches must admire the lion's roar, for they seem to try to imitate it. African travelers say they do it very well, too. Hunters can be sure of one thing. A roar at night means a lion; a roar in the daytime an ostrich.

Did you ever see a cat miss catching a mouse? She looks ashamed of herself. She peeps around to see if any one noticed her failure, and slinks away as if she wanted to forget it. Lions do the same. And they do not attack elephants and other big, thick skinned, tusked animals that fight back. Nor do they attack men, unless they are wounded or driven into a corner, or sometimes when the man is asleep and helpless and the lion very hungry. Some African travelers say that if a man meets a lion, all he has to do is to stand still and look him square in the eyes and Mr. Lion will back away, then turn tail and run. I wouldn't like to put that to the test, would you? But a lion is used to seeing animals run from him in fear. It might puzzle him to see a man stand still and stare at him. Wild animals are a good deal like human beings in that. They are afraid of what they don't understand.

Travelers say the lion isn't nearly so brave as the tiger, nor so noble as he looks. He slinks along through tall grass, or behind bushes with his head hanging below his shoulders. He never fights any animal that can defend itself unless he is forced to do so. The only time he shows great courage is in defending his mate and cubs, and then the lioness is fiercer than the lion. In captivity, of course, he is savage. He thinks of himself as in a trap, very likely, and that every man who comes near him wants to kill him. That makes him very dangerous.

How do you suppose this big, bearded wild cat is ever tamed so far that he lets his trainer use him for a pillow, drive him to a cart, play see-saw with him, wrestle with him, and jump through a hoop at a word of command?

The training of a lion is simple. He has to be made to understand two things. One is that his trainer is his friend and means to use him well. The other is that the man is master. The trainer begins by going up near the bars, talking to the lion kindly, and throwing him some meat. It isn't long before the lion learns to know and to watch for the man who feeds him. Next the trainer, while talking, puts a stout stick between the bars.  With a terrible roar the lion springs on the stick and crushes it into splinters.  But the trainer keeps right on putting sticks between the bars, talking kindly to the lion and feeding him.  After a few weeks the lion pays no attention to the stick, or he smells it and walks away.  Finally he lets the trainer touch him with it, and stroke his back as he eats.

It is several months before the trainer tries going into the cage. He takes the stick with him and a stout chair.  He sits down and pretends to read a newspaper.  The lion crouches back in a corner and growls.  If he should spring the trainer has the chair up, legs out, before his face, and Mr. Lion gets a bumped head and a blow on the nose—his tenderest spot.  Very slowly he learns to trust his master and to fear him, too.  Sometimes a lion seems to grow fond of his trainer.

When petted he will purr as if he had a whole swarm of bees in his throat.  But trainers never forget that the tamest lion is always dangerous.  He is sly and treacherous, too.  Without an instant's warning he may forget all his lessons and turn on his best friend. So the trainer watches and watches, never quite trusting even a lion that he has brought up from a cub.

Lion cubs are the cunningest babies.  They really look and act more like puppies than kittens.  They are as fat and clumsy and woolly as Newfoundland puppies.  In Lincoln Park Zoo, Chicago, a keeper takes a family of three or four lion kittens out onto a grass plot for a romp.  Crowds and crowds of people watch them tumble over each other.  They are not born blind as tame kittens are, but they are just as helpless, and for a long time cannot even lap milk from a saucer.  Sometimes the mother lion, soured on the world by being shut in a cage, won't have anything to do with her babies. They die unless some other animal with milk can be found to nurse them.  The very best foster mother for lion kittens is—not a cat, but a dog.  A shepherd or collie dog is the best, for she is trained to care for sheep.  She nurses them, fondles them and seems as proud of them as a mother.  But in a few months they grow so big and rough that she looks at them in wonder and alarm, as a hen looks at a duckling she has hatched to take to the water.  She must think the fairies have changed these babies in their cradles, for they are none of hers.  And by the time they are old enough to be weaned they are too much for doggie.

# "Here Come the Elephants"

That is what the children shout when a circus parade marches through a town. The elephant is the children's delight. Draped in purple and gold he walks with the tread of an emperor before a conquered army. All the other wild beasts are in cages, but he, the largest and strongest of them all, a three-ton mountain of an animal, is led by his keeper as if he were a big-good-natured dog. And oh, if there is a baby elephant the children just about go crazy.

No wonder! Baby elephants are scarce. Even in her home on African plains, or in the East Indian jungle, a mother elephant has a baby only once in ten or fifteen years, so there are never more than a few babies at a time in a big herd of a hundred or more elephants. It's a great event when one is born in captivity. Such a baby! He weighs two hundred pounds at birth, is nearly three feet high and has a funny little trunk about as long as your twelve-inch ruler. And you never saw such a baby for growing! At the age of one year he weighs half a ton. When he is hungry he squats in front of his mother, spreading his hind legs out behind him, pokes his head up between her *front* legs and sucks milk with his mouth, just like a calf. She pets him with her trunk while he nurses, and she doesn't wean him until he is two years old.

A baby elephant is as solemn as an Indian papoose. But in his own clumsy way he is very playful. He plays hide-and-seek between his mother's legs, and pulls her foolish little tail with his trunk. When anything alarms him, he gets right under her and shuffles along that way. And when she crosses a stream he climbs on her back until he learns to swim. In one thing he doesn't get over being a baby until he is a grandfather. He spends half his life cutting new teeth. An elephant has twenty-four grinding teeth in all, but he cuts and uses only four at a time. As one set wears down a new set appears just behind. Maybe it is cutting teeth that makes a big, fifty-year-old elephant peevish, sometimes.

There is a secret that a very young baby elephant can tell you that even his mother doesn't know. Ages ago there were elephants and mammoths and mastodons that were much like them, only twice as big as any elephant living today. They lived all over Europe and America, some of them away up in the coldest countries where

385

NORTH AMERICAN ANIMALS

1—Mountain Goat. 2—Rocky Mountain Sheep. 3—Bluebird. 4—Wild Turkey. 5—Raccoon. 6—Pronghorn. 7—Bald Eagle. 8—Bison. 9—Prairie Chicken.

SOUTH AMERICAN ANIMALS

1—Vampire Bat. 2—Howling Monkey. 3—Aracari. 4—Condor. 5—Opossum. 6—Toucan. 7—Tanagers. 8—Tufted Hummingbird. 9—Peccary. 10—Llama. 11—Pampas Deer. 12—Agouti. 13—Guinea Pig. 14—Ant Bear. 15—Pampas Chicken. 16—Rhea. 17—Jaguar. 18—Diamond Snake. 19—Pitted Frog. 20—Swimming Marsupial. 21—Armadillo. 22—Scaly Salamander.

polar bears live today. They were covered thick with wool and hair, and had long hairy manes like those of the buffaloes, falling over huge curved tusks twice as long as a tall man. Today, you know, elephants haven't a sign of a hair on them. Their thick gray hides are as bare as rubber blankets. But baby elephants, when first born, have a scanty covering of silvery brown wool all over their pink, piggy skins. That tells very plainly of a time when all elephants had fur.

It takes an elephant thirty years to grow up to eleven feet in height, twelve in length, with tusks and trunk six or eight feet long, and a weight of three tons. He has plenty of time, for, if he is lucky, he may live to be a hundred or more years old. The hide of a full grown elephant is an inch thick, and full of folds and creases and wrinkles. The ears of an African elephant are as big and floppy as rubber door mats. He can smell as well as a dog or a bear, and see and hear much better. His legs are as thick and solid as the pillars under a portico, and his feet are scolloped with five thick toes around a pad. An elephant's knees and elbows are so near the ground that it is hard for him to get up and down. He can't curl his legs under him as many animals do, but kneels and sprawls his hind legs out behind. Sometimes he seems to say: "What's the use in trying to lie down at all?" So, when he is sleepy, he just leans up against a big tree, or a rock. And he has a stiff neck all the time. His neck is so short and thick that it is very little use for turning, although he can toss his head up and down like a bull.

For such an enormous animal the elephant is wonderfully active. He can shuffle along, in his clumsy way, nearly as fast as a horse can run. East Indian elephants climb steep mountains as pack animals, and are very sure-footed. All elephants are good swimmers and hard fighters if attacked. They can charge the enemy like cavalry horses. Their tusks are terrible weapons, and no other animal living has such a wonderful tool-chest as the elephant's trunk. It is a nose to breathe and smell with, an upper lip, a finger and thumb, a stout arm, a water tank, a club to fight with, and a musical instrument all in one. As hollow as a garden hose, that trunk is made up of forty thousand muscles laid length-wise, cross-wise and on the bias, in a net-work that gives it great strength and variety of motion. With its trunk the elephant can pick up a peanut, pet its baby, pull a small tree up by the roots, give itself a shower or dust bath, break off a leafy branch and shoo away the flies, slap

Father, mother, and baby African elephants. The father's trunk is raised, and you can imagine hearing him trumpeting. African elephants are larger than their Indian cousins, and have much larger ears.

This Indian elephant has just picked up a peanut thrown to him by children and is rolling it with his trunk to his mouth.

390

# Elephants at Work

Photos by Ewing Galloway, N. Y.

a saucy tiger senseless, and bellow like the bass horn in a brass band.

But *why* is it called trunk?

Don't you suppose nearly every little boy and girl in the world has asked that question? And got an answer something like this: "Oh, just because it is." But that is no answer. The name is really *trompe*, a French word meaning trumpet, for the trumpeting sound the animal makes. English people misunderstood the word and changed it to trunk. Besides it looks like the stem or trunk of a small tree turned upside down; and there is a hollow tube for forcing pellets through, something like a pop-gun, that is called a trunk. So trunk seems just about as good a name as trompe, doesn't it?

Elephants live in herds like buffaloes. There are from twenty-five to one hundred in a herd. They wander about together in the woods and on the open plains of Africa and India, wherever there is plenty of grass, low plants and trees, near water. They sleep in the forest. As early as three o'clock, long before the sun rises, a herd is on the march. They go in single file, the big bulls in front breaking a path through the thickest jungle. Then come the cows, and last the mothers with babies. This is the order in which Indians travel, the warriors ahead and the children in the rear.

If danger threatens, the bulls trumpet a warning. All the others stop, and the bulls line up to give battle to the enemy. Some people think that only the flesh-eating animals are dangerous. This is a mistake, as you must know when you remember how savage some bulls of domestic cattle are. African bull elephants are so fierce the lion tucks his tail between his legs and slinks away, when he hears one trumpeting. The tiger sometimes attacks the smaller East Indian elephant, and often gets the worst of it.

African explorers and travelers say a charging bull elephant is a grand and terrible sight. He blows his mighty trumpet in a blast that can be heard for miles, lowers his head with its six foot tusks, and tosses his trunk up out of danger. He knows how easily that precious member, all delicate muscles and nerves, might be injured by claw or spear. When a tiger springs, the bull catches him on the tusks, tosses him twenty feet in the air, gives him a swinging blow with the trunk as he comes down that stuns him, then pins him to the earth with the tusks, or tramples him under his three tons of weight. It is said that every pair of tusks brought out of Africa has cost one or more human lives.

Usually a herd marches to the feeding ground unmolested. There they pull the grass up by the roots, beat the earth off on their front legs, give the bundles neat twists, and poke them back into their mouths. They pull up bushes and break off high leafy branches. They even uproot small trees, prying with the tusks and pulling with the trunks. Cocoanuts are cracked and shelled by rolling underfoot. They are fond of palm nuts, sugar cane and yams, a kind of sweet potatoes. In captivity elephants are fed on hay and carrots, but they just love peanuts, popcorn and candy. A herd of one hundred wild elephants will eat ten tons of food a day.

About sunrise the whole herd takes a bath. They go on a shuffling run to the nearest "ole swimmin'" hole. Into the water they go up to their eyes. They frolic like so many school boys, shouting at the tops of their—trumpets, slapping and splashing water over each other. The babies ride on their mother's back, slide off and learn to swim. Often a herd plays in the water for an hour. Before coming out they suck up as much as ten gallons of water each, through the hollow trunks and stow it away in water pockets in their stomachs. Later in the day, when they want a drink or a shower bath, they bring this water up and use it. The camel seems to be the only other animal that has storage tanks inside for water.

Old hunters in Africa and India say members of a herd look alike as do members of a human family. Some herds are made up of animals that are large and strong and bright minded. In other herds the animals are smaller, weaker and more stupid. In East India the natives speak of elephants as low caste and high caste, and say there is as much difference as there is between breeds of dogs and horses. And no hunter will go after a "rogue" elephant. A "rogue" is a tramp elephant. For some reason he has left his herd, or been driven out. No other herd will admit him, so he turns sour and becomes very dangerous, fighting every living thing he meets, and destroying what he cannot eat.

Elephants hate flies. The flies and stinging insects of hot countries are large and thick and tough as is the elephant's hide they manage to get into the folds and creases and sting him. He fights his tormentors with shower and dust baths and fly brushes. When they drive him frantic he rushes into the water to wash them off. There he finds a friend. It is the long-legged water crane who stands on the elephant's back and picks out the flies to eat. Sometimes this feathered friend and a baby elephant may both be seen riding on Mother Elephant's back.

Of two things the elephant is afraid—fences and mice. A fence looks like some of the traps used by native tusk-hunters. The flimsiest fence of reeds, bamboo or barbed wire will usually keep a herd of hungry elephants out of a sugar or yam field, or will keep them prisoners inside a stockade. As for a mouse, very likely the elephant thinks it a big insect that will run up his trunk. He throws the trunk up out of danger, bellows with rage and trembles with fear.

The huge African elephant is very wild, hard to tame and teach, and is of uncertain temper. Even the cows have tusks. A good specimen is not often seen in a menagerie. The East Indian elephant is smaller, more easily captured and tamed. He readily learns to do useful work and to perform tricks. He becomes fond of a kind master, and likes children, dogs and peaceable animals. He is not brighter than the dog, but because of his size and strength and his wonderful tusks and trunk, he can do a great many things that a dog cannot do. In India, the elephant piles half-ton teak logs in lumber yards, and is used in the timber and stone work of roads and bridges. He can push a cannon across a bog, carry a load over a mountain, and help sporstmen hunt and kill tigers. East Indian rulers all have troops of elephants to use in warfare, and to ride in royal processions. In Siam, the white elephant is a sacred animal and has a place on the national flag.

How old and wise the elephant in the menagerie looks. It is very comical to see such a heavy, clumsy animal stand on his hind legs or his head, dance to music, blow a horn, beat a drum, ring a bell or fire a gun. He kneels to let children and dogs and monkeys climb into a canopied throne on his back, then rises and takes them for a ride. He plays see-saw with another elephant, forms pyramids, rolls barrels, piles boxes and does many other hard things. The elephant has a good memory. He never forgets a trick he has once learned. He remembers an unkindness for years, and is sure to watch patiently for his chance, and to take terrible revenge on a keeper who mistreats him.

Hundreds of years ago the Greeks and Romans trained elephants to perform in their open-air circuses. Ancient writers tell of elephants that rocked cradles of babies whenever they cried, and of others that walked and danced on tight ropes. One writer says that elephants were sometimes found practicing their tricks at night, because they liked to do them, perhaps, or because they had been punished for not performing properly and wanted to know their lessons better. That seems hard to believe, but some trainers of today say they have watched these huge animals saying over their lessons out of school.

Wild elephants are sometimes captured in herds, and tamed. The hunters build a great stockade of log posts standing about ten feet high after they have been driven in the ground. Other logs are laid crosswise to the posts and lashed firmly to them. A large gate is left open. Then the beaters surround a herd and slowly drive it toward the stockade, often taking weeks at this work. Finally the herd comes to the gateway and enters the stockade. The men close the gate. Now comes the schooling or taming of the herd. Tame elephants are mixed with the herd, and in a few months the wild elephants have learned to like their trainer and know how to live and do the work for which they are trained.

Don't you think these clever animals deserve all the petting and peanuts they can get? Some elephants will eat right out of a child's little hand. But you should always ask his keeper if it is safe to feed an elephant in that way, and what he likes best. And be very careful not to touch his precious trunk.

Courtesy of The American Museum of Natural History

# The Animal Acrobat and Clown

Can you think of anything that will collect a crowd of children so quickly, or keep them happy so long as an organ grinder with a monkey?

The music is often very dreadful, but the monkey is very funny. His tiny wrinkled face is so comical. It looks like that of a wise little old man who has seen a lot of trouble. Like a good clown in a circus, a monkey doesn't have to do anything to make people laugh—except just *be* a monkey. He is so wonderfully agile, quick and clever. He mimics everything people do. He "makes faces," he dances to music; he runs up the telegraph pole, a tree or a porch pillar, and he swings from bars like a trapeze performer. He picks up pennies, stuffs them in the pocket of his absurd red jacket, and pulls off his collar-box cap for thanks.

It seems a pity that a monkey can only chatter or scream or scold, for he tries ever so hard to talk. Such a mischief he is, too. If he sees a chance he will snatch a little girl's doll or a lady's hat and tear it into pieces. He knows very well such behavior is naughty, for he scrambles out of reach of punishment, and chuckles with glee over the trick. It's easy to forgive the little rascal, for the next instant he does something engaging. He cuddles his baby, or cracks a peanut like a squirrel, turns a hand-spring for you, or slyly pulls another monkey's tail.

Just what *is* a monkey?

In the big cage in a menagerie or zoo, there are a dozen or more varieties of monkeys as unlike each other as a fox terrier is unlike a St. Bernard dog. Some monkeys are as small as chipmunks, and others are as large as cocker spaniels. There are monkeys with long curly tails, with straight tails, bushy tails, stub tails, and no tails at all. Some have very hairy, and other nearly naked faces. There are dog-faced and purple-faced monkeys; monkeys with white cheeks, with turned-up noses, with tufted ears, with whiskers, mufflers and bonnets. Most of them are black, gray or some shade of brown, from silver-fawn to seal. But there are dandified monkeys with green coats and orange vests.

Many people call all the big apes—the gorillas, chimpanzees, orang-utans, baboons and gibbons, monkeys. But we won't do that. These huge, man-like creatures from the Old World are savage, and have to be kept separately in strong cages like other wild beasts. They are hard to catch, hard to tame, and harder to keep alive in captivity, so you will not often see one. By monkey, children always mean one of the smaller apes that can be tamed easily and led about by a string like a little dog, or kept with many others in a big room of wire netting and bars.

A monkey in captivity is happier in a cage with a number of other monkeys. "The more the merrier" is the rule in monkey land. Nearly every kind of small ape lives in a monkey village in the trees, when he is at home. There is a wise old male for a chief. He and the older males keep trespassers away from a chosen feeding place, and he leads them to a new home when they move. Early in the morning and late in the evening, seems to be play-time in a monkey town. All the monkeys leap and swing and chase each other, and "whoop and holler" as Riley says, like so many boys playing in the woods. Spoiled boys they are, too, doing a great deal of mischief by throwing down cocoanuts and other fruits and nuts, just to see them fall.

Some of these monkeys have the prettiest homes! They camp out all the year round. They love the dense woods of very hot countries. In the beautiful tropical forests along the Amazon River, in South America, monkeys live in bowers in the trees, among red and green parrots, butterfly orchid blossoms, brilliant birds and insects and flowering vines. They live in thousands of tropical islands in the sea, among palms and fruit trees. But a few are found in colder countries: in Mexico and in the mountains of India, Japan and Northern Africa, and even around the great fortress rock of Gibraltar, in Spain.

No matter how much monkeys may differ in other things, they are all alike in having four hands. The bear, the lion, the elephant, the dog—nearly all the animals you can think of, have four feet. Little girls and boys have two hands and two feet. A foot has a long sole and short toes, usually, and the toes cannot grasp and hold things. A hand has a nearly square palm, fingers much longer than toes, and a thumb. In the best kind of a hand the fingers and thumbs have three joints each, and can all be brought together in many positions, and even closed into a fist. All four of a monkey's feet, that he walks on, are really hands, with grasping fingers and more or less perfect thumbs. That is why a monkey is so clumsy on the ground. Usually he walks on the outside edges of the palms with the fingers and thumbs curled in. This gives him a funny, bow-legged look. But just watch him on a tree or a perch, or clinging to the wires of his cage. He's as much at home in a tree as a bird or a squirrel.

Even if a monkey cannot talk, he can tell you very plainly where he lived when he was at home—that is, whether he is an Old World monkey from over the ocean, or a New World monkey from South America. The monkeys in a zoo always come to the netting when visitors appear, for they are very curious and want to see every-thing that is going on. Besides, they have learned that some 'specially friendly little boys and girls carry bags of peanuts. Select any little fellow who comes up to you and give him peanuts, one at a time, as fast as he can take them. If he is an Old World monkey he will stow those nuts away in cheek pouches like a squirrel. He can put a surprising number away, for those pouches stretch and stretch like little rubber balloons. Look at him carefully. His nose, of course, is flat, but the two holes are near together. And when he goes up to a bar to eat his nuts, he does not use his tail in climbing.

A South American monkey's nostrils are far apart. He has no cheek pouches, but heaps as many nuts as he can carry in his two front arms, as you carry packages. But he can keep other monkeys from taking his nuts when he climbs, for he uses his long, curly-tipped tail for a fifth hand. With five hands for grasping the South American monkey is a wonderful trapeze performer. The tree-squirrel climbs faster, the flying squirrel leaps farther, the bat clings better with his wing-hooks, but no other animal can climb, leap and swing, and go across a wide forest, forty feet from the ground without once coming to the earth. The acrobat of the animal world, he seems to be made up of wire springs that are tireless.

The South American monkey that you will see oftenest with the organ man is a small, rusty brown animal about as big as a toy terrier. He has a curved hair-covered tail, good thumbs, a rather pleasant whistling chatter, and a care-worn anxious face, as if he expected nothing in life but bad news. He is bright and obedient, so he soon learns his tricks and performs them willingly. He likes to ride on a dog's back, his master's shoulder or the barrel organ. Another favor-ite of the organ man's is the Capuchin (Cap-u-chin) monkey. You may know him by the queer way in which the hair grows around his face like a hood or Capuchin monk's cowl.

MOUNTAIN GORILLA

WHITE-FACED CHIMPANZEE

RHESUS MONKEY

JAVAN MACAQUE

398

HUMBOLDT'S MONKEY

OWL MONKEY

GOLDEN MANTLED MARMOSET

WHITE-FACED SAPAJOU

Photos, New York Zoological Society

Sometimes in school you learn a rule, and then the teacher will tell you that there are times when the rule doesn't work. The marmoset, the smallest and prettiest of all South American monkeys, cannot use his tail in climbing. When children see the marmoset they always cry: "Oh, what a little dear!" He is no bigger than a chipmunk. He is only eight inches long, with a furry body and a foot-long bushy tail that he carries like a plume. If it wasn't for his almost human little face and hands, and his wing-like, tufted ears, you might think him some kind of squirrel.

There is a squirrel monkey from South America only a little larger than his nut-cracking namesake. He has a gray face and a black nose, but has long hind legs so he leaps something like a kangaroo. When he is happy he shows it by grinning, and when he is hurt tears come into his eyes. In his home in the Amazon forests it rains torrents sometimes, as if the bottom had fallen out of the clouds. When caught in such a storm, a troop of these squirrel monkeys huddle together in the thickest tree they can find, and put their tails around each others' necks for company and comfort.

These marmosets and squirrel monkeys have some of the noisiest neighbors—the howling monkeys. They begin howling at sunrise, keep it up until the next sunrise, and then take a fresh start. The woods ring and echo with their howls. They travel all the time through the high branches of the trees, the males leading, and the mother monkeys following, each with one or two babies clinging to her neck with fingers and tails. They swing by their tails and catch the next limb with a hand. The brown howler is bad enough, but the red howler makes the night hideous with his cries. They screech as if all the animals in the forest were eating each other up. Some zoos won't have Little-old-man-howler, as he is called, at all.

Another South American monkey is the Saki. He has a ruddy back, and an almost human habit of cupping a hand and dipping up water when he wants to drink. He is so delicate that he seldom lives long in captivity, so you may never see him. But you are sure to see the spider monkey. He has such long slim arms and tail, and such a small body that he looks like a big, hairy spider. But really he is very gentle and even affectionate. He has little stumps of thumbs that are of little use to him, and he is not as agile as many other monkeys. A mother spider monkey likes to sit down and cuddle her baby in her arms.

So many of the Old World monkeys have only little stubs and lumps of thumbs that scientists put them all into one family called the colobus or cut-off-thumb monkeys. If you see a monkey with a very fine, long-haired silk coat, particularly if he has cheek pouches and makes no use of his tail, look for shrunken little thumbs. His coat makes pretty monkey-skin collars and muffs. One colobus of the mountains of Abyssina, where it is cold, looks as if he were wearing furs himself. He has a fringe of white down either side his jet black body, a white tippet under his chin, a white edge to his cap and a white tip to his tail.

Another colobus of the hot west coast of Africa wears the hair on top of his head in a crest, with a parting on each side, something like grandma used to comb your daddy's top hair, in a long fat curl called a "roach." This crested colob looks very comical, indeed, for, beside his roach, he has whiskers under his chin. A near neighbor of his in the African jungle is the "face-maker." He is a very good tempered, teachable little fellow. The variety of queer faces he car make always draws crowds, so he is a favorite with the organ man.

Among the brown and gray and black monkeys in a zoo, you will be sure to notice many that are brightly colored. There is a red and a purple-faced monkey; a Diana monkey, with a pretty white crescent like a new moon on the forehead, a white beard and neck scarf, and a monkey with a blue mustache above yellow whiskers. He is called the mustache monkey. The green monkey is quite a dandy. He is dressed in dark green and black, set off with dull orange whiskers, throat band, breast-plate and tail-tip.

At first sight the Hanuman monkey of the East Indies doesn't look especially interesting. He is a little grayish-brown, spider-legged animal with black hands and face. But he is a privileged being. In his native land he is sacred to Hanuman, a monkey-faced god. He is never interfered with, so he goes in troops into the villages, helps himself to grain, friuts and nuts in shops and houses, and destroys things from wanton mischief. The people of India are so kind to all living creatures that several "bad boy" monkeys are very troublesome. Stories are told of a whole tribe of the Hanuman or Rhesus monkeys swarming into dining rooms and eating wedding feasts. Another mischievous monkey is the magot who lives in Northwestern Africa, and in Spain around Gibraltar. He is about as big as a terrier dog. He and all his relations go to a fine garden and set sentinels in trees and on rocks to watch, while the others eat and destroy melons, figs, grapes, oranges and almonds. An alarm sends them flying. This bad habit lands many of them in zoos and traveling shows, because traps are set for them.

The street strollers of India, Japan and Northern Africa lead about the macaque (ma-cake') or bonnet monkeys. The hair of the macaques grows in a frill around the face. These sunbonnet babies are quick and clever. One of them loves crabs so well that he has learned to swim and dive for his favorite food. The pig-tailed bonnet monkey of the East India Islands is used on plantations to climb up the tall palms, where men cannot go, to pick cocoanuts.

Now there is one very sad thing about these amusing little creatures, or rather there used to be. Tropical animals, as most of them are, they very seldom lived over the first winter in our colder country. Like human beings they often caught tuberculosis or pneumonia, or some other lung trouble, and died. Steam-heated houses were built for them to live in, in the winter, and every breath of cold air was shut out. They seemed to die all the faster. Mr. De Vry, the animal keeper in the Lincoln Park Zoo of Chicago, thought he would try the fresh-air treatment on the monkeys. One fall he fed his monkeys even more good food but left them out of doors. See what happened.

They shivered and had to jump around very lively to keep warm. But the monkeys lived and thrived. Their bodies grew fat, their furry coats long and thick.

In the cage were several mothers, each with a baby cuddled in her arms. Never before had a baby monkey been born in captivity in a cold climate. They lived, too, and frisked about as if they were in the hot forest along the Amazon, instead of on the bleak shore of Lake Michigan.

MULE COLT
AND MOTHER

SHETLAND
PONY AND COLT

# The Ship of the Desert

There is one baby animal that rides when he goes bye-bye. He isn't carried on his mother's back, or in her breast pocket. He rides in a hammock on the back of a trained nurse. Something dreadful would happen to that nurse if he should stumble and drop the baby. Its mother follows close behind them all day, watching with her big brown eyes. The owner of the animals watches, too. That is a precious baby. If he lives to grow up he will be worth as much as a fine horse.

It is the baby camel that rides in this way. Although he is three feet high, and heavier than a bossy calf when he is born, he is so weak and wobbly on his legs that he can scarcely walk. Without his mother's milk he would die. The mother has to go with the caravan of hundreds of other camels. A caravan, or passenger and freight train of camels, travels fifty or more miles a day across the burning sand and rocky hills of the deserts of Sahara and Arabia. So the helpless baby camel is put into a hammock, and swung from one side of a big, two-humped freight camel. The nurse may carry half a ton of other things besides,—leather bags of water, bales of cloth and dates, jugs of oil and blocks of rock salt. All day long the nurse swings along at a rocking gait. The baby must feel much as a human baby feels when rocked in a cradle.

There is a curious reason why the baby isn't put on his mother's back. Camels are very stupid animals. If the mother could not see her baby, even if it was on her own back, she would be apt to think he had been left behind. Then she might turn and bolt for the last camping place. On the nurse-camel she can see him, and she follows contentedly.

A camel isn't really a wild animal, and he isn't really tame. He is too stupid to be either one or the other. For many hundreds of years the camel has been one of the most useful animals to men, because of his great strength, and his endurance of heat, thirst and hunger. But he has never learned to do more than a few simple things. He never seems to know or to care for his driver, or for a master who may have brought him up from a baby. He looks very wise and meek and good-tempered. But really, he has as little sense as a sheep, is as ill-tempered as a cross bull, and as stubborn as a

↑

## A FREIGHT TRAIN OF THE DESERT
A caravan of camels carrying spices, silks, rugs and other merchandise.

**The camel driver** with his pair of "desert ships" is resting in a market place. Notice the star-like ornament the front of the saddles.

**This camel waits** patiently while ↓ his rider, an Arab Moslem, faces toward Mecca at time for prayer.

mule.  He works, but not willingly, as a horse does.  If he had as good a mind as the elephant, no man could make him work at all.

In the hot, dry desert regions the camel is the horse, the cow and the sheep of the Arabian herders and traders.  He carries all the burdens, he furnishes flesh and milk for food, and hair for weaving cloth.  To the children of America the camel is as strange and interesting as many of the fiercest wild animals.  We know less about him than we do about bears.  He tells you very little about himself, and he shows no curiosity about the crowds that visit his pen at the zoo.  He gazes over people's heads in a dreamy way, just like that old stone sphynx head that stares across the desert in Egypt.  One bright little boy once said: "A camel is like a great, big jigsaw puzzle."  Let us see if we can work out a little of this living puzzle.

Don't go too near a camel's head.  Sometimes, for no cause at all, he has a terrible fit of rage.  Then he tries to bite and to kick the person nearest.  The first thing you are sure to notice, and to laugh at, is the queer way in which he chews his food.  His lower jaw swings from side to side like a hammock.  His upper lip is cleft up the middle.  It is what is called a hare-lip.  The camel stretches and twists and feels its food with this thick, split lip as if it were two fingers.  He doesn't seem to look at his food at all.  So you are quite ready to believe he has never learned not to eat poisonous plants that grow on the desert.  A herd of browsing camels has to be watched as close as a flock of silly sheep.

Everything about a camel is as queer as if you had dreamed him in a nightmare.  His neck and legs look too long and sprawling for his body.  His feet are split into two hoofed toes almost up to the ankle.  His head is too small, and is tipped up and poked out in a foolish sort of way.  His long brown eyes fairly pop out of his head like agate marbles, from sockets too small for them.  His nostrils are bias slits.  He can open them wide or close them almost shut.  His rough, red-brown hair looks as if it never had been combed.  On his knobby knees and elbows and arched breast-bone he wears bare, leathery pads like a football player.  Finally, his hump makes him look as if he had his back up against an unfriendly world.

One of the few things the camel has learned to do is to kneel when he is ordered to do so.  At a word he drops.  The pads protect his joints from the hard ground.  He moans and groans as if in terrible pain.  He knows some kind of a load is to be put on, and complains aloud.  He doesn't wait to find out if the load is to be heavy or light. He carries half a ton of goods for hundreds of miles across wide deserts, with ease. But he groans just as loud when he is asked to carry two little children about his track in the zoo. With more groans he heaves his big body up and starts to run, or rather to rock.

If you get sea-sick on a boat you would better not try to ride a camel. He lifts both feet on one side at the same time, tilting his body sideways. Then he lifts the two feet on the other side. So you roll over and back. Tossing and pitching, heaving and rolling you go, as if you were in a sail-boat on rough water. In a minute you are sick at the stomach. Very soon your back aches from the jolting, and you get a sharp pain at the waist line. Maybe you think this is why the camel is called the Ship of the Desert. It isn't. It is because he carries people and goods across wide seas of sand.

Haven't you heard people say: "Handsome is as handsome does?" If you could see the camel at home where he "does handsome," you would forget what an ugly, ungainly beast he is. You would think how wonderfully he is made for the work he has to do. No other animal can live and carry great burdens in such a climate, on such scant supplies of food and water.

It is a wonderful thing to see a camel caravan start from a town on the edge of the desert. There are hundreds of animals in a great yard, tons of goods in bales, dozens of drivers and passengers, and a swarm of dogs. The owner of the caravan is a white-robed and turbaned Arab chief. He looks over every animal carefully. There are slenderly built racing dromedaries, or one-humped camels, with hair so fine that it is used for making artist's paint brushes and dress goods. And there are stout, short-legged, two-humped freight camels as shaggy as bears. Indeed, there are as many breeds of camels as there are of horses. The fleetest of foot can travel a hundred miles a day, the slowest only twenty-five.

The first thing the owner looks at is the hump. No camel is taken with the caravan unless its hump is big and solid. The hump is the camel's pantry shelf full of fat, to be drawn upon when food is scarce. Next, the feet are looked over to see that there are no stones between the toes, and no thorns or bruises in the soft foot-pads. Just before starting the animals are given all the water they can drink. A camel can drink enough water to last him three days. His second stomach is a honey-comb of little tanks for storing water.

The passengers, the chief, and the women and children of his family mount the dromedaries. Half a ton or more of goods, the leather water bottles, oil jugs, tents, sleeping rugs, bags of dates and beans to feed the animals, and the baby camels in their hammocks, are loaded on the stout, two-humped camels. The drivers and herders walk, and the dogs tail in at the end of a mile-long procession. At the front ride the chief and his sons, or helpers. They carry guns, for there are robber bands on the desert—regular train-robbers who "hold up" rich caravans, and steal goods and trains also.

The start is made very early in the cool of the morning, while the stars are still shining. There is no roadway or trail. The sand shifts and drifts like loose snow before every wind, filling up tracks as fast as they are made. A camel caravan travels as does a ship at sea. It is guided by the sun and the stars, and by certain hills, rocky gullies and dreadful heaps of bleached bones.

In the hottest hours of the day there is a rest for men and animals; at night a long rest. Tents are put up and animals are unloaded. A camp is set up under date palms beside a well. Every foot of hundreds of camels is examined. A torn or bruised pad is cleaned, dressed with healing salve and tied up in rags. The animals are hobbled by strapping one hind foot up to the knee, so they cannot stray.

For food, after a day's travel, a camel is given a small measure of hard, sugarless dates or dry beans. Besides, he crops leafless twigs, thistles and thorny shrubs. Camels will eat anything. They will chew their own leather bridles, or tent cloth. One witty writer has said that a camel can make a breakfast from a Sunday newspaper and an old umbrella. He can go without water for three days.

Day after day a camel caravan travels in this way, covering hundreds of miles, and touching at lonely green islands of oases. Sometimes a great wind storm sweeps over the desert, hiding the sun and filling the air with a blinding, stinging rain of sand. Down the animals drop, under their loads. They stretch their necks out straight, shut their eyes, close their nostrils to the narrowest slits, and lie still. The people turn their robes over their heads and huddle in the shelter of the loaded humps. Above the roar of the wind and the hissing and pelting of sand and pebbles, can be heard the low moaning and hard breathing of the camels. They seem to suffer. Yet, when the storm is over, they rise and rock on as before, across the burning waste.

Although the Bactrian or two-humped freight camel is a native of the high, cold plains of Central Asia and North China, he thrives and works just as well in the heat and drought of the desert. In his old home he is a draft animal, too. He carries burdens over snow-covered plains and even mountains. He sleeps out of doors on the snow in gales of icy wind. He eats, not only hard, bitter plants, but fish, bones and tough skins. He can go for a week without water, and when no other is to be found, can drink the salt, bitter waters of dead seas. On the desert he can carry heavier burdens and endure greater hardships than the one-humped dromedary, although he is burdened with an arctic coat of wool and hair. He is the ox of the earth's waste places, as the dromedary is the riding horse.

At night, when a caravan is in camp, the little children of the chief drink cups of the camel's thick, cheesy milk mixed with water. On the chief's table is camel flesh, as juicy and tender as beef. The herders wear robes and turbans of brown, camel's hair cloth. The master sleeps under a camel's hair tent. Without this ugly, stupid, useful beast, the hot deserts of the Old World would lie unpeopled and unknown. The camel knows nothing of his value and cares less. Like the desert itself, he submits to be used, but remains wild. Sullen and forbidding, he holds his master a stranger.

There is just one thing for which the camel has a softer feeling. The mother camel shows affection for her baby. After the day's march she has him all to herself. She nurses him, she nuzzles him with her sensitive hare-lip. He cuddles up to her for warmth. After the terrible heat of the day the night on the desert is often cold. But it is very still and clear. She can feast her eyes on her baby, for the dark, blue-velvet dome of the sky is hung all over with little golden lamps of stars.

Opossum, showing young at the mouth of the pouch.

Opossum, showing young on the mother's back. —→

"Playing 'Possum." This animal is alive. ↓

By Ewing Galloway, N. Y.  SPIDER REPAIRING WEB

Underwood-Stratton.

**A Beaver Uses His Sharp Teeth To Cut Down Trees For Building Dams.**
He has a broad, flat, muscular tail, covered with skin-scales, not with hair.
He uses his tail as a prop when he sits upright, and as a rudder and oar when
he swims. To send a danger signal to other beavers, he slaps his tail loudly
on the surface of the water.

# Kangaroo and 'Possum, Too

If you like to be surprised, all of a sudden, just stand by the kangaroo pen in a park zoo awhile.

You are sure to wonder, at first, why there is such a very high, strong fence of iron posts and netting around these queer-looking animals. No taller than kindergarten children, they sit upright as neatly as if on three-legged stools. You might say they *are* three-legged stools, for kangaroos rest on two hind legs and a long fat tail. From these broad bases their bodies taper up in the oddest way, to narrow, sloping shoulders and small, deer-like heads. Their full bright eyes glance about, their rabbit-like ears stand erect, listening. In front of the breast the short fore-paws are drooped, as if they are there less for use than for ornament.

Sometimes the kangaroo drops on all fours and eats like a rabbit, hopping about on his hind legs like a robin. But it seems to be easy for him to pick up a carrot, hold it between his paws and eat like a squirrel. The keeper knows what he is about when he scatters the food, putting some choice bits in the farthest corners of the pen. He does that so you can see the animals—*jump!*

There! You nearly jumped out of your skin, didn't you? That's surprise number one. When a kangaroo wants to go across his pen he doesn't waste time in hopping. He just stretches up on his hind legs and leaps. If a frog was as big he might jump farther than a kangaroo, but he couldn't jump as high. It really must have been the kangaroo, and not the cow, that jumped over the moon and made the little dog laugh.

No wonder the kangaroo can jump so far and so high. He has the biggest and strongest hind legs, for his size, of any animal in the world. His hind feet are so long it looks as if he were sitting on his hind elbows. At the end of the foot is the biggest big toe! It is in the middle of the foot, and has on it a long, sharp, wicked-looking, dagger-like claw. On one side of this big toe is a small one. On the other side a pair of helpless little twin toes dangle from the leg. The kangaroo's hind leg, foot and big toe are as wonderful, in their way, as the elephant's trunk.

A long, long time ago, when there were big, fur-covered elephants on the earth, there were also kangaroos as big as hippopotamuses, with heads three feet long.    Perhaps it was these huge jumping beasts that started the story of the giant, who wore seven league boots and could step over small mountains.    Why, a kangaroo six feet high of today can leap over a horse and rider, and then get away by jumping as fast as the horse can run.

These queer animals live in only one place in the world—the big island continent of Australia, away around on the other side of the earth.    Living on grass, small plants and the roots of herbs, they take the place of the deer and antelopes of other countries. Like other grass-eating animals they live in herds with leaders, and are naturally very timid and peaceable.    There are a dozen varieties of kangaroos.    The largest are as tall as a man, and weigh one hundred and fifty pounds.    The smallest aren't as big as a rabbit.    Some live on wide plains, some in the mountains and other climb trees and feed on the leaves.    Like antelopes, they bound away on the slightest alarm.    If overtaken and attacked, they will fight.    The giant kangaroo can kill a man or a dog with one slash of the big-toe claw.    A horse it will puzzle and frighten by jumping over it and back again. A small dog that annoys it, the animal is said to pick up in its forepaws, carry to a nearby pond or brook, and hold under the water until it is drowned.

Here is another odd thing.    When feeding, two or three little ones follow each mother in the herd, hopping around her.    On the slightest alarm the babies vanish!    Not one is in sight as the herd goes bounding away.    The little ones are not on their mother's backs, and there are no holes in the ground big enough for them to go into.

Watch the kangaroos feeding in the zoo, and maybe you can solve the puzzle of the disappearing babies.    There doesn't seem to be a baby in the pen.    Suddenly a little head, no bigger than a mouse's head, pops out of the fur on a mother's breast, like a jack-in-the-box, and pops back again.    That is surprise number two.    The mother kangaroo has a deep, flat, fur-lined pocket on her stomach.    You never suspect such a thing because she can shut the top as tight as your mother can snap the clasp of her shopping bag.    She can open it, too, for the little ones to jump in and out.

Kangaroo babies need that pouch.    When they are born they are only an inch long—about as big as June bugs—and blind, naked and helpless.    They cannot even suck their mother's milk, as kittens and puppies can.    Their mouths fasten over the nipples inside the bag, and the mother *pumps* milk into them every so often.    They

AUSTRALIAN ANIMALS

1—Koala. 2—Bird of Paradise. 3—Kangaroo. 4—Emu. 5—Marsupial Wolf. 6—Cassowary. 7—Lyrebird. 8—Talegalla Hen. 9—Helmet Cockatoo. 10—Frilled Lizard. 11—Duckbill. 12—Ant Porcupine. 13—Nymph. 14—Owl Parrot. 15—Kiwi. 16—Nestor Parrot. 17—Ceratodus.

## AFRICAN ANIMALS

1—Gorilla. 2—Chimpanzee. 3—Banana Bird. 4—Aye-aye. 5—Ringtail Lemur. 6—Mandrill. 7—Hippopotamus. 8—Giraffe. 9—Ostrich. 10—Kudu Antelope. 11—Jacko Parrot. 12—Elephant. 13—Rock Rabbit. 14—Guinea Fowl. 15—Wart Hog. 16—Lion. 17—Chameleon. 18—Shorthead.

live in the bag for months, scarcely moving. The first time they come out they must climb up and tumble over the edge of the fur pocket, like little birds leaving the nest. For a long time afterwards they sleep and travel in the pouch. It is a sort of dining and sleeping car to them, and a nice place in which to play hide and seek.

There is only one other animal in the world that has a pouch just like the kangaroo's  Curiously enough this little cousin of the Australian kangaroo lives in the southern part of the United States, and doesn't look much more like him than a cow looks like a camel. He is about twenty inches long and has a body much like the body of the 'coon or little tree-bear. He lives in trees, too. Little boys—especially little colored boys—down South, often catch him when he is a baby and bring him up for a pet. He's the cunningest, brightest little fellow, with one trick that you like to copy.

Did you ever "play 'possum?" You shut your eyes and pretend you're asleep, for a joke. The opossum does this in earnest, to make an enemy think he is dead. He fools the dogs of hunters, sometimes, by rolling up into a limp ball and lying still. But a pair of bright eyes are watching out of the fur, and when the dogs are off guard, the 'possum unrolls and slips away.

The opossum doesn't jump like the kangaroo. All four of his legs are the same length, with five-clawed toes for climbing. He doesn't walk very well, and takes to a tree as quickly as possible. His dingy white or gray fur is tipped with brown all over, so it is not easy to see him in a tree. He has a long, scaly tail like a rat's, but he can use it as a monkey uses his tail for climbing and swinging. He has the sharp, pointed face of a big rat, the naked ears of a bat, the five-clawed feet of a little bear, and the pouch of the kangaroo. He makes his nest in the hollow of a tree like a bear, but he doesn't leave the babies at home. Mother 'possum carries them in her pouch when they are small. There are a baker's dozen of them—that's thirteen—and they are only half an inch long when they are born. She cares for them as the kangaroo mother cares for her babies.

When 'possum babies are big enough to come out of the bag—oh, about as big as mice—they like to ride on the roof of the car. There are so many of them that part of the family climbs on the father's back and part on the mother's. The babies sit in a row, clinging fast with their claws to the fur. The father turns his long tail over his back, clear to the head. The babies wrap the ends of their little tails around his tail, and away they all go for a stroll.

The 'possum is a night prowler. On still, bright, moonlight nights whole 'possum families are out in the fields, woods and swamps hunting for berries, nuts, grain and roots. They eat insects, field mice, little squirrels and birds' eggs, too. But, best of all, they love the sweet, frost-wrinkled fruit of the persimmon tree. This weakness for persimmons often gets the little family in trouble. Sometimes they are caught in a tree by hunters with dogs.

Usually they get away in safety. On an alarm—just a rustle in the grass, the distant bark of a dog, or the smell of a man or gunpowder, the babies pop into their mother's pocket. The whole family scampers back to the home tree, and slips, in two packages, into the grass-lined nest in the hollow trunk.

Really, that nursery pouch idea is so clever, that one wonders why only the kangaroo and his little American cousin, the opossum, are provided with them.

# The Graceful Giraffe

If anyone ever held his head high in this world it is Mr. Giraffe. If you could keep him for a pet he could easily poke his head in at a second-story window, and wake you up in the morning. He could stretch his tongue out, quite two feet, and lick your face, or twist it around a curl and pull your hair with it. And, if he would let you, you could climb out of the window onto his head, and toboggan-slide down his neck and back almost to the ground. You would have to put a feed box on the roof of the barn for him, and give him plenty of hay, corn, grass and carrots, or he would eat the tops of the shade trees. Maybe he would eat them anyhow, for he likes juicy green leaves that he pulls himself, better than anything else.

Guess what kind of an animal the giraffe is. Don't be ashamed if you can't guess. The Arabs on the desert, who have known him longest, gave it up long ago. They named him *Xi-raph'a*, which means graceful. A name that merely tells what a thing looks like is no name at all. Besides, the giraffe isn't a graceful animal. The Greeks, who were a very wise people, made another guess. They called him camelopard (ca-mel'o-pard) because, like the camel, he has a long neck, and his coat is spotted something like the leopard's. Really, the coloring and markings of the giraffe are more like those of the baby deer. The Greeks may never have seen the pretty spotted fawn of the Northern forest, or they would have noticed that. The stretched-up neck, and small, arched, gazelle head of the giraffe are not at all like the thick, bent-down neck and tipped-up face of the camel. Let's look this queer animal all over and see what he is like.

He has the beautifully shaped, split hoofs and the slender legs of the antelopes, but the legs are so lengthened that his body appears to be lifted on stilts. His shoulders are so high that his fore-legs look longer than his hind legs, although they are the same length. He has a short brushy mane, from between the ears to the shoulders, like the zebra, and the zebra, you know, is a small striped wild horse. He has the fly-whipper tail of the ox. Isn't that a mixture? But there's more to this living puzzle.

The giraffe's lustrous brown eyes are like those of the woodland deer, in beauty and gentleness, but they are set out from the head even more than the camel's eyes. Indeed, the giraffe can push his eyes out sideways, as if they were on stalks, and look around behind him without moving his head. Wouldn't he make a grand school teacher? No other animal has eyes just like the giraffe's, and no other grazing animal has an eighteen-inch long, barbed rubbery tongue that he can stretch up another foot, twist around a bunch of leaves and pull it down. It is something like the tongue of the ant-eater or honey-bear. In just two things the giraffe is like the camel. He can close his nostrils against blowing sand, and he can go a long time without water. This is not because he has water pockets in his stomach. He simply seems to need much less water than other animals. Finally, the giraffe's long neck, high shoulders and short body, that form one curved slope from ears to tail, are quite unlike those of any other animal on earth. He is three times the height of a six-foot man, and towers five or six feet above the biggest African elephant.

As an animal, the giraffe is half-way between the ox and the deer. He is most nearly related to the antelopes, of which there are forty varieties in Africa, from the pretty, graceful gazelle to the gnu, or horned horse. But, unlike the ox, deer or antelope, the giraffe has neither horns nor antlers. The two, solid, bony growths on his head are covered with skin and hair, and are topped with tufts of bristles, comically like a pair of daddy's shaving brushes. The giraffe's leg bones are solid, too, while the large bones of all other grazing animals are hollow in the middle. Now, do you know what to call him? "Mr. Graceful Camelopard" is a misfit. He seems to have kept this name only because no other has been found that suits him any better.

Giraffes are very hard animals to find and to capture. Like the true antelopes they are less savage than they are timid. Very wild and shy, they trust to their heels for safety. They live in herds of from a dozen to fifty on the high dry plains of Central Africa, below the desert and east of the tropical forests. Their only enemies are lions, who lie in wait for them in the brush along river banks, and Arab hunters on horses. They are much brighter than camels. Two or three of their number always stand sentinel, while the others feed. This is very necessary, for the tall giraffes are shining marks in an open country. Their short-haired skins ripple and shine like satin with every movement, and in the sun the colors brighten to orange-brown and cream. In the shadow the colors fade and darken to sandy-fawn and seal brown.

A sentinel giraffe stands on the outpost of a herd, among the trunks of a clump of thorny mimosa trees, his head just peeping above the crown of leaves. Among the small trees his legs are not noticed. His body appears to be a part of the dancing leaf-shadows and sun-spots. His head, eighteen feet in the air, topping the low growth of the plains, with the open ears, keen nose and stalk eyes, makes a fine watch-tower. It isn't easy to take a herd of giraffes unaware. The only chance the lion has of catching one, is to spring on him while drinking. Even then a giraffe has been known to kick a lion to death. With five minutes' start the swiftest Arabian horse cannot overtake a giraffe.

If closely pursued, a giraffe can escape through a jungle of thorn bushes where men on horses cannot follow, and come through without a scratch. His skin looks to be thin and tender, but it is really so tough and so thick in places that soft lead bullets often flatten out on it. If cornered, the giraffe kicks like a mule. Dr. Livingstone, the African explorer, says a giraffe's kick is as bad as a clap from the sail of a Dutch wind-mill. The animal fights with his head, too. Having no horns, tusks, or antlers, he does not lower his head and charge, like a bull elephant or buck deer. He gives a long, swinging blow sideways, using his head and neck as a sort of hammer, and striking with his powerful lower jaw and teeth.

As a rule the giraffe keeps out of trouble by running away from it. In running he has three gaits. He rocks like a camel with his neck stretched out; he trots like a horse with his head held high, and he gallops or bounds like the antelope, but more clumsily, his long neck plunging up and down with every bound. Because of his long stride he can get over the ground as fast as a horse, but he tires sooner.

Most giraffes in menageries and zoos are caught young. A mother has only one baby at a time, an ungainly spotted calf that is almost as helpless as a baby camel. When the herd is alarmed and starts to run a baby may be left behind and be captured. Full grown giraffes are sometimes caught with the cow-boy's lariat, but there are few rough riders who can throw a lariat loop twenty feet high and drop it over a giraffe's head. Great care must be taken to give the plunging, frightened animal plenty of rope, or he may give a sudden jerk and break his long neck.

In his book on hunting in Africa, which you should read, President Theodore Roosevelt said giraffes don't always run when men come near.  He got very close to a cow giraffe that had her head in a tree taking a nap.  So it seems, the giraffe, like the elephant, sometimes leans up against a tree to sleep.  The animal looked at him sleepily a moment and closed her eyes again.  As he came nearer she kicked at him.  When the rest of the party came up and threw sticks and clods at her, she showed her teeth in an ugly snarl, like a cross dog.  Finally she kicked out at them and then trotted away.

Of all the large animals in a menagerie or zoo, the giraffe worries his captors and keepers most.  His neck is so long it is always in danger of being broken.  He has to have an open sky-light in the roof of his cage to put his head and neck through.  Sometimes, in turning around in his small cage, the neck is twisted or a bone snapped.  In traveling on a railway, the roof window has to be kept shut, or the first low bridge would catch the head of the animal.  He is not ill-tempered, as a rule, but having his eighteen feet of height jammed under a ten-foot roof makes him peevish.  Sometimes he refuses to eat, and sometimes he turns vicious and attacks his keeper with his hammer of a head.  So, although he looks so gentle, with his mild and beautiful eyes of a deer, you should never go very near a giraffe's cage.

But you should never miss a chance to see one of these strange and interesting animals.  Like the bison, or what we call the American buffalo, the grizzly bear, the African elephant, the Bengal tiger, the kangaroo, and many other wild animals, the giraffe has been hunted so long that he is rapidly disappearing.  A hundred years from now the children may be able to see only stuffed giraffes in museums of natural history.  They will think how lucky the children of our day were to see these queer beasts alive.

# Mr. Nose Horn and Mr. River Horse

"How do you say them? And which is which?"

That is what the very little boy asked about the rhinoceros and the hippopotamus when he came home from the London zoo. Their dreadful names made his head ache, and he couldn't tell them apart. He was sure children could have made up much better names for animals.

"Well, why is a dog a dog?"

"It isn't," said the very little boy; "it's a bow-wow." His daddy laughed, for he was a very bright daddy and saw the point. And then he told the very little boy that a great many things seemed to have been named, as a baby names a dog "bow-wow," by something about them that a child would notice first. Once upon a time, perhaps, a hunter in Africa or India, came upon two strange beasts. They both had enormous bodies on very short legs, and they both liked to wallow in the mud. When he went home he wanted to tell his friends about them so they would know the animals, too, if they ever saw them. One he called Mr. Nose Horn. That is, if he had been an Englishman, he would have said nose horn, but as he was a Greek, he said rhino-ceros, which means the same thing. The most striking things about the other animal was its huge horse-like face, and its habit of living most of the time and feeding in the water. So he called that animal hippopotamus (hip-po-pot-a-mus), two Greek words meaning river-horse.

No child could have made up simpler names than those. But, oh dear, when you come to study these queer animals it does seem that those wise old Greeks might have found better names. If they had thought of the shape of his body, his short legs, his rough, thick skin, of how he likes to wallow in a mud puddle and then go to sleep in the sun, of his four-hoofed toes, and of his sword tusks like those of wild boars in German forests, they would have called the hippopotamus the water-pig. And if those old Norsemen who used to roam over the northern seas in big row boats had seen the animal, these are the things they would have noticed: He can stay under water from five to eight minutes, he spouts when he comes up for air, his naked skin is oiled so he can slip through the water easily, and under that skin is a thick layer of solid fat.

The hippopotamus has a body as long as the elephant's. It is from ten to fifteen feet around the middle, but the animal's thick legs are so short that he stands only five or six feet from the ground. Really his legs are better for swimming than for walking. He has the small, dull eyes of the pig sunk in folds of skin, small ears, a wrinkled, scowling forehead, a mouth two feet wide, and a bulging upper lip. He can use his sharp-edged tusks for rooting and for fighting, as the wild boar uses his tusks. He has a mustache of feeler hairs on his upper lip—like a cat? No, it is more like the bristles around the mouths of some whales—especially baby whales. But he doesn't breathe through holes in his head and spout water when he comes up to breathe, as the whale does. He has nostrils like other land animals. When he dives, he shuts his nose holes to keep out water, as the camel and giraffe shut theirs, to keep out sand.

Like other hoofed animals, the hippopotamus lives in herds and feeds on plants. From two to three dozen live together on the banks and in the beds of the warm rivers of Africa. They are not so bright as elephants, neither are they stupid. Not more than one or two of a herd are ever caught in the same kind of trap. Where hunters are about, the hippopotamus does not snort and blow when he comes up to breathe. Sometimes a herd leaves a place that is much hunted. They are rather timid and peaceable animals. When they hear a sound, or smell something they do not understand, they sink under water with only their noses above, and stand motionless, hidden among water plants. Maybe you have seen mud turtles do the same thing.

If attacked, a hippopotamus fights ferociously. A big bull hippopotamus will swim under a boat and tip it over, or bite a big piece out of the side, with his huge bark-cutting teeth. He chases the men in the water and gores them with his tusks. There are terrible "rogue," or tramp hippos, too, as there are among elephants.

A mother hippopotamus is the fiercest of all, if anything threatens her baby. She has only one at a time, and she makes it her chief business to look after him. He isn't born a swimmer, so for a long time he lives mostly on his mother's back. If caught young the baby hippopotamus is easily tamed, but he isn't bright enough to learn tricks. When his keeper comes to his cage he opens his two-foot wide mouth and begs for food in the most comical way. He asks for it much as a pig does. At home a herd of hippopotamuses at play shout with loud, harsh voices, but in a cage they creak and groan and squeal like very rusty hinges of a door.

When a herd of hippopotamuses in the Nile River becomes tired of a diet of water plants, it climbs up higher and steeper banks than you could climb, breaks into fields and eats wheat and sugar cane. Just think of having a drove of animals in your corn field as big as elephants with their legs sawed off, with stomachs that hold five bushels, and with the table manners of pigs! Then, sometimes, they like to plaster their red and brown and gray-splotched, hairless bodies with mud, and go to sleep in the sun just like pigs. The only thing that will keep them out of a field is a bonfire. Practically all wild animals are afraid of fire.

It is the rhinoceros, or nose horn, that ought to have *hippo* (horse) in his name. He is a very distant relation of the horse. He has teeth like a horse and a three-toed foot as horses once had. No horse or his near relatives, the zebras and donkeys, has a horn. So, perhaps, you will not be surprised to learn that a rhinoceros' horn isn't a horn at all. It is more like a corn.

This is the difference: A tusk is an overgrown tooth, a horn grows from the bones of the head, a finger nail is a sort of horny substance that grows from the flesh, a corn is a thickening of the skin. You get a corn on a toe where a shoe rubs or pinches. In rooting about for his food, or in fighting, the rhinoceros may have bumped his nose and kept on bumping it until a "corn" grew there. That "corn" is really a tuft of stiff bristles cemented together with a kind of horny glue. Around the base of it the thick hide grows in leathery folds, and the outer layer of the "corn" often peels back in shreds, like the rough bark fibre on a cocoanut shell. If you watch a rhinoceros in a cage, you may see his nose-horn move when he wrinkles his thick lip and forehead.

Except that he is a huge, nearly hairless beast who likes to wallow in the mud and water, the rhinoceros is not in the least like the hippopotamus. His legs, while thick, are longer, and lift his body higher from the ground. His head tapers to a pointed muzzle, and he has the upright, nervous ears of the horse. A regular wild horse in armor he is, for his thick, leathery skin is laid on him in folds that overlap at the natural joints of his body. Having such a weapon right between and below his eyes, the rhinoceros doesn't miss many chances of using his nose-horn. He doesn't avoid trouble like the timid hippopotamus.

The rhinoceros is a grazing animal, too, but does not find his food in the water. He feeds by night on wooded hillsides, in the brush or on swamps, and uses his nose-horn to pry up roots and his horse teeth to bite off grass. During the heat of the day he often takes a cool bath and rolls in the mud. Very likely he goes into the water many times for the same reason as the elephant. He is tormented by flies and stinging insects. Like the elephant he, too, has a feathered friend. Isn't it odd that the rhinoceros bird should also have a nose-horn? He is Mr. Horn Bill. This bird travels around on the animal's back and picks the insects out of the folds of skin. He has that choice feeding ground all to himself, for the rhinoceros baby doesn't ride on its mother's back. Father pushes the baby along in front of him with his horn, as if he were in a baby cab, on wheels.

The rhinoceros can hear and smell well, but, like the hippopotamus, his small eyes are very dim. The bird on his back often gives him the first warning of danger by uttering a loud cry. At that the animal plunges into the brush or makes for the nearest water. He can out-run a horse, but he doesn't run away, as a rule. He merely chooses his own place to fight. He runs into a pool or river, rolls in the water and heaves up, his sides dripping

Ten feet long and seven high, with a dagger-like curved weapon three or four feet long on his nose, the bull rhinoceros is a monster. He tosses his huge, horned nose, sniffs and snorts and lowers his head for the charge like a wild boar. Knowing that he sees badly and charges straight, a skilled horseman can dodge him. A lion leaps over him, tucks his tail between his legs and sneaks away. An elephant that stands twice as high, often weighs but very little more, and is no match at all for this big brute. The rhinoceros can run his nose under the elephant's body and kill him with his dagger horn.

Thousands and thousands of years ago enormous hairy rhinoceroses with two nose-horns and shaggy manes, roamed over all the colder parts of Europe and America with the giant hairy elephant. The bones of a great many of them have been dug up on the banks of the Upper Missouri River. Just think! Enormous two-horned and two-tusked woolly beasts, bigger and fiercer than any elephants and rhinoceroses of today, may have uprooted trees and cropped wild grass on the very pasture where your pretty Jersey cows eat clover. He was once an American!

RHINOCEROS, PHOTOGRAPHED EATING HIS DINNER

MR. and MRS. HIPPOPOTAMUS PHOTOGRAPHED FROM LIFE

# Wild Animals Near Home

Do you live on a farm? Or in a small town with woods and fields around it? There is a creek, perhaps, a swamp, hillside pastures, stone or rail fences bordered by briars. Then you have animal neighbors as wild and shy as any you will see when the menagerie comes to town. Take a long tramp over the country after a light snowfall. Don't take a dog with you. Take an opera glass, a microscope and a camera. Walk in the face of the wind, or all the little wild creatures will get early news of you and vanish.

Watch for foot-prints—trails of tiny tracks in the snow. Those are calling cards. Some nature-lovers can read every kind of track as easily as you read print. They can tell where a rabbit has gone across country by long jumps, and sat on his haunches in places to "stop, look, listen!" They can tell where squirrels have played tag around a tree; where field mice have chased each other around a straw stack; where muskrats have come up the bank of a frozen pond; where a chipmunk has sunned himself on an old stump lookout.

There are very few places in America where some of these rodents —little gnawing animals—are not to be found. But city children often know the common gray squirrel and the little brown chipmunk, better than country children do. That is a pity, for where they are not hunted all our native squirrels become very tame.

In a city park if you sit on one bench day after day and scatter peanuts or popcorn near you, the squirrels will learn to come to be fed. They leap on the bench, by and by, eat from your hand and go into coat pockets for nuts. Be patient at first, and keep wide awake, or you will miss seeing little switch-tail when he slips, a gray shadow, down a tree. Flash he comes, stops, "freezes" on his haunches, bright eyes watching, ears and plume up. Shelled corn scattered about a farm or country school yard will coax him out of the woods. Don't try to catch him or he will never come back.

What a pretty little fellow! All silver-gray, brownish-gray or even black, he is, for squirrels of the same family vary in color, just as foxes do. A little ten-inch furry bundle of fun, with a ten-inch banner of a tail! He plays tag, leap-frog, runs races on walls, rolls up and coasts down hill. He is just as curious about you as you are about him. He is very gossipy, chattering all day, but he attends

A WHITE RABBIT.

MOTHER RABBIT AND HER BABY HAVING A LITTLE SIESTA
IN THE WARM SUNSHINE.

ALLIGATOR

WOOD TURTLE

BADGER

AMERICAN TOAD

WHITE-FOOTED MOUSE

429

GREEN FROG

FLYING SQUIRREL

# Animals
# Near Home
# In Woods
# Fields
# And Rivers

BOX TURTLE

PORCUPINE

OTTER WITH FISH

to business, too. If he is hungry, he will sit up and show you how to crack and eat a nut. Then he will carry away what you give him, one nut at a time, and bury each, lightly, in a separate place. He will come back for them, by and by, and carry them into his high pantry in a tree.

On a snowy morning his foot-prints will guide you to his elevator door, the foot of a tree. Sometimes he uses a hole for a den, but often a crow's nest hammock, roofed over with leaves and bark. He cares neither for cold nor wind. His nest blown down by a gale, he catches on a limb like an acrobat, or drops on his feet like a cat. After eating he washes his face like a cat.

For the underground burrows of the chipmunks, look in the deepest woods, around old stumps, logs and boulders. Look sharp. Tail and all, the chipmunk is less than a foot long, and he is just the color of rotten wood. Even the black and white stripes on his back are mere lights and shadows. A sunny, woodsy streak, he flashes across the open, stops stock still, upright, alert, and is gone. You are not sure you saw him at all. Perhaps you heard his gleeful "chip, chip, chip!" It is a challenge. He would just as soon lead you a merry chase as not. Little soldier, every log is a breastwork, every stump a sentry box, every screen of undergrowth a retreat. And for all he burrows, he is not a true ground squirrel. He can climb, and his habits are those of the tree squirrels.

With a last saucy "chip!" he is gone. Find his house-door, if you can. He hides the little round hole cleverly among drifted leaves, shaded by ferns and moss. You will find his snug den below frost-line, leaf-bedded and stored with acorns, nuts, and red winter berries. But you will not find the owner at home. He has another house or two just like it, and his bright eyes may be watching you a few yards away.

No country in the Old World has so many true ground squirrels as we have. Prairie dogs, gophers and woodchucks are ground squirrels. The gopher is the ill-tempered, rat-like hermit of the garden. You may be sure he is under a flower or vegetable bed, biting off roots, if plant tops suddenly wither. But be careful in digging him out. He cannot be tamed, and he bites with his chisel teeth. The prairie dog is found only on the wild plains of the West. To try to dig a village of these amusing little yappers out is like starting to dig a well. In the park zoo the prairie dog village is in a deep cement-lined pit filled with earth, so these clever little animals cannot tunnel and spread over the park.

You can dig the woodchuck, or ground-hog, out. He is the fat, sleepy-head bear squirrel. Don't look for him in the woods. Keep your eyes open when crossing a hill-side clover field, or in going down a steep creek bank. If you see a hole big enough to thrust your arm in, probe it with a stick. If the hole slants upwards, Mr. Woodchuck is there. In the winter you can dig him out and roll him on the snow, like a flabby muff of coarse, gray-brown hair. He is so fast asleep that if you take him into a warm house he will open his eyes, yawn, crawl under a bed or bureau, and go to sleep again. Some people say he wakes up on the second of February. If the sun is shining, and he sees his shadow, he knows there will be six weeks more of winter, so he goes to sleep again. With his clumsy body, flat head, beady eyes, and small ears and tail, he doesn't look in the least like a squirrel. But he sits upright to eat, and to look about. He never goes far from his hole, for he cannot run well. When alarmed, he jumps to shelter like a rabbit.

Molly Cottontail pricks up her nervous ears at that. "Not run well! Just watch me for three seconds!" she says. Look out for bunny. She is the color of dead grass, weeds and snow. She may be at your feet, or in that weedy fence corner. She smells you, hears you, sees you. She doesn't know yet, whether to sit still or to run. Boys can't smell rabbits, but dogs can. "Zip!" there she goes, a flying brown shadow, the bit of white under her tail, a flag of truce that no one regards. Poor Molly Cottontail! A timid, helpless creature, her only safety is in her legs. She cannot climb a tree, dig a den, or bite. She cannot crack nuts nor store food. She can run fast but not far. Her home is wherever she sleeps, out in the open, ears erect, eyes half-closed, nose wide and quivering. She is lucky if she gets forty winks at a time. If no dogs are about, she may creep under a barn, or in a wood pile, in cold weather. She distrusts a hole, because foxes, owls and other enemies live in holes.

The one clever thing she can do is to cut tunnel roads in undergrowth. Bunny slips and winds through these six-inch mazes of runways she has patiently cut with her teeth. There she puzzles and tires out dogs and foxes by crossing the scent, and so gets away. A sociable little creature, Molly lives a fugitive life and all alone, for safety. On some brambly hill-side, you may come upon the shallow nest she has scooped out and lined with white fur from her own breast. Do not frighten her. There she brings up her brood of six or eight babies, in fear of their lives and her own.

MUSKRAT

GOPHER

PRAIRIE DOGS

MOLE

WOODCHUCK OR GROUND HOG

WEASEL

By Ewing Galloway, N. Y.

RACCOON

Photograph from Underwood & Underwood.

MINKS

Allan D. Cruickshank from National Audubon Society.

SQUIRREL

American Museum of Natural History—New York.

COYOTE HOWLING NEAR TREE

American Museum of Natural History—New York.

CHIPMUNK

American Museum of Natural History—New York.

SKUNK ON GROUND

RED FOX

By Ewing Galloway, N. Y.

When crossing a field in winter, stop and listen at hay and straw stacks, and shocks of corn fodder. On the stillest, frosty day you may hear a crisp rustling within. Look all around for the tiny, bird-like tracks of field mice. Most field mice make beds in the ground and sleep all winter, but others stay awake. They are the bed-makers of our wild life. They can make a warm bed of anything —leaves, grass, corn-silks, feathers. Up in the woods you can find the tiny trails of the fawn and white-deer-mice, and find their feather-lined nests in rotten stumps. You will know them by their big ears and bright black pop-eyes. Certain mice tunnel around pits of potatoes, beets and cabbage. They store clover and other roots in earth pockets. In countless hidden places out of doors these busy little gnawers have nests of babies no bigger than thimbles.

The mole you can always find by the long ridge of cracked earth that zig-zags across fields—the roof of his tunnel. It is lively work to dig out a mole, for he may be at either end, or anywhere along the route, or in a side chamber. If frightened by the noise you make, he will go deeper and bore a yard in ten minutes.

In your hand he lies helpless, a flat ball of fine, velvety, mouse-colored fur, six inches long. He has no neck or ears, dim pin-points of eyes, and a naked, pink tail that looks like a short, fat earthworm. Put the sprawly, wiggly creature on the ground. He scrambles about frantically until he finds a soft spot. Then he begins to bore with his bony gimlet of a nose. With his spade-like fore feet he digs and pries the earth back. In less than one minute the animal has disappeared. Do not kill moles. They are insect eaters. Mice, ground squirrels and rabbits are root eaters. The mole goes through the earth and around roots, eating slugs and beetles.

In the story of "Big Brother Bear," and in the main part of this book you can read about the raccoon, or little tree-bear. And in "Kangaroo and 'Possum, Too," you can read about the opossum who has a fur pocket on her stomach to carry her babies in. These animals are found only in the South, as the prairie dog is found in the West. Every part of our country has some special small, wild animal—mink, weasel, badger, fox, skunk—whose haunts and habits are interesting. There is just one more that is found all over the United States, wherever there are creeks, ponds and swamps. This is the muskrat.

You can scarcely go skating on a frozen pond in the winter without finding a dome-shaped, mud and grass house, or a little village of a dozen homes frozen in the ice and covered with snow. Mr. Sharp, a nature writer, said that you can skate all around them and sit on one to strap your skates, without bothering the furry bunch of sleepers inside. But push a stick carefully through the thick wall and you can hear a soft skurrying inside, then a "plunk, plunk, plunk!" as one after the other plunges into the water, through a doorway below the ice.

The muskrat doesn't mind. You couldn't wet his sleek, brown fur coat any more than you could wet a duck's feathers. He only sleeps in the daytime, in winter. Each stout dome has a single-room. It is a sort of club house, or European hotel, where a number sleep in one bed, snuggled up to keep each other warm. At night they all tumble out into the icy water and hunt for food. They dive for fresh water mussels, and bite off tender white calamus blades. You know how good calamus is. They bring their food up through a hole and wash it, just as the 'coons or washing-bears do. After this feast of a sort of oysters on the half-shell and celery, they often go up into orchards for frozen apples—fruit ice. A dainty feeder is the muskrat.

The muskrat builds his house only for a winter sleeping place. In the summer he burrows in the bank or builds under bushes on the swamp. Mr. Burroughs said he is a fine weather prophet. If he begins to build by October—and he works only at night—you may be sure there is to be a cold winter. Or, if he builds very high and strong, his house solidly plastered to logs, stumps or tussocks of grass, look out for high water.

A dark lantern, with which you can throw a light over a pond, will give you glimpses of muskrat families feeding. Only a foot long, their fur is so thick, rich and glossy a brown that it is sold as river mink. Muskrats sit up to eat, something like squirrels, or rather like kangaroos, using their six-inch flat scaly tails for third legs. They use those tails for rudders in swimming, too, and with them they slap the water to warn others of danger. Perhaps, who knows, they use them as beavers use their tails, for trowels in plastering their houses with mud. For his size the muskrat is just as bright and clever as his big cousin, the beaver.

Even where they are too quick, and you fail to see them, you can tell where muskrats have been by a faint musky odor, as of a flower perfume on the frosty, moonlit air of a lonely marsh.

## HUNTING WITH A CAMERA

Hunting with a camera, by day or with flash-bulbs by night, is often more fun and more challenging than hunting with a gun. When people are friendly, wild life will come into wood lots and back yards. Birds will come to back-yard feeders in winter. Where houses are not too close together, near areas where deer abound, deer will come to feed in-fields and woods when they know that guns will not crack.

# Your Dog

AMERICAN
COCKER SPANIEL

If you try to understand the wishes of your dog as well as he tries to understand you, you will have happy times with him.

People have always had dogs for companions in work and in play. Mongrels, or dogs of mixed breeds, may be good pals. Some breeds of dogs do certain kinds of work better than other dogs.

Toy dogs make good pets for indoors. Sporting dogs, hounds, and terriers are useful for hunting game birds and various kinds of animals—even people and objects that are lost.

Some of the larger non-sporting dogs and working dogs are good lifesavers. For a long time large working dogs have been used for herding sheep, goats, cows, pigs, and reindeer. Some are so strong that they pull heavy fishing nets. Others pull loads of food and supplies on sleds and in carts. Many breeds of dogs are good for guard or patrol duty.

To keep well and happy, children need plenty of fresh water to drink between meals, and good nourishing food. So does your dog. Many dog owners feed their dogs a good prepared dog food that provides the kinds of mixed diet that dogs need most. It is not good for a dog to overeat. A dog needs a comfortable, dry place in which to sleep. You should brush and comb his coat and give him plenty of exercise each day.

Sometimes, dogs need to be wormed, or to have distemper or rabies inoculations. It takes patience and kindness to train a dog to be well-mannered.

## ———SPORTING DOGS———

CHESAPEAKE BAY
RETRIEVER

WELSH
SPRINGER
SPANIEL

Pictures by Courtesy of KASCO MILLS, INC.

438

# MORE SPORTING DOGS

POINTER

IRISH SETTER

## HOUNDS

AMERICAN FOXHOUND

GREYHOUND

BLOODHOUND

# MORE HOUNDS

SMOOTH DACHSHUND

WHIPPET

BEAGLE

# WORKING DOGS

DOBERMAN PINSCHER

NEWFOUNDLAND

STANDARD SCHNAUZER

Pictures by Courtesy of KASCO MILLS, Inc.

SHETLAND SHEEPDOG

ESKIMO

GREAT DANE

SPITZ

ST. BERNARD

ALASKAN MALAMUTE

# AND MORE WORKING DOGS

SAMOYEDE

BOXER

ROUGH-COATED COLLIE

# TERRIERS

SCOTTISH TERRIER

SEALYHAM TERRIER

IRISH TERRIER

AIREDALE TERRIER

WIRE-HAIRED FOX TERRIER

# TOY DOGS

PEKINGESE

POMERANIAN

MALTESE

# NON-SPORTING DOGS

BOSTON TERRIER

BULLDOG

CHOW CHOW

DALMATIAN

# Art Through The Ages

These pictures in "Art Through the Ages" have been selected for children to see, to have explained to them, and to enjoy. Thus they will come to feel that art of all ages is a part of their lives. Their enjoyment of the pictures will lead to curiosity, and their curiosity will develop an ever-increasing appreciation of higher forms of art from childhood throughout life.

In each historic period, the art that was produced was new in its own time. It was new because it was being made by living persons.

Art is what people make. So every child, every adult, is an artist. Art has always given form and color to what people make and do, so that their everyday living may be more spiritually and physically satisfying and fruitful. Art creates our tools, homes, clothing, furniture, dishes, ornaments, statues, pictures, music, literature, and all things about us. We even speak of the "art of living" when we mean a harmonious way to think and act and conduct our lives.

When a baby reaches his hands to touch something, he is beginning to become an artist, for he is learning of the forms and textures of objects, as well as of colors. He is also beginning to find enjoyment in what he sees and feels. Curiosity leading to action is the child's pathway to the ability to do things. The instincts leading to actions are nature's way of guiding children happily into the knowledge of things. Children need to touch, feel, handle, and play with things. Only in this way may they learn how to do and make things, and to develop their personalities and understanding.

A story lies behind each piece of art. It may be the story of a need for a tool, a home, a church, a school, or an automobile. And it may be the story of human yearning to catch forever, in paint or metal or stone, the form and personality and character of children and adults, and of the harmonies on land and sea and in the sky.

444

# Earliest Forms of Art

The earliest pictures and carvings that we know were discovered in caves in southern France and northern Spain. They were colored drawings of the animals shown in the above picture. Thousands of years ago people of the Middle Stone Age painted these pictures with grease and earth on the rock walls and ceilings of their cave homes.

Among the first objects made by primitive peoples were the tools that they used to obtain food and clothing. They made these tools of bone, horn, and whatever else they could find. In time they learned to make decorations on their tools so each person could know which were his.

Over the years they became more skillful in their arts as they continued to carve their tools and decorate their homes and fashion their clothing. They made more beautiful patterns and colors.

On this page you can see pictures of some objects that were made long ago. The rod of authority was carried by the head man of a tribe to show that he was the leader. A pebble was put in the child's hollow clay toy so that it would rattle when the toy was shaken.

445

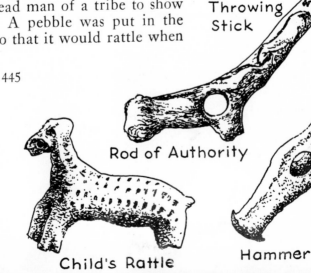

Bone Knife

Flint

Throwing Stick

Rod of Authority

Vase

Decorated Bone

Child's Rattle

Hammer

# Ancient Egyptian Art

The dry climate of Egypt helped preserve early works of art. The Great Sphinx is the largest portrait figure ever made. It portrays the head of King Khafre (Kăf'rā) on the body of a lion. Some of the tombs of the rulers were made in the form of pyramids. The inside walls were covered with pictures such as the one shown below, which tells the story of the harvesting of wheat. In drawing the human figure, Egyptian artists showed the head, arms, legs, and feet sidewise. But they drew a front view of the eye on the side of the face, and a front view of the shoulders on the side of the body. Large statues of the ruler Ramses II were placed between pillars at the temple at Luxor. Examples of jewelry, spoons, furniture, mirrors, and pottery of his time are preserved.

446

Egyptian Tomb Wall Painting

The Sphinx, Cairo

The Discus Thrower
The Met. Mus. Art

# Beauty of Grecian Art

When the early Greeks first visited Egypt, they imitated the art of the Egyptians. Later Greek sculptors and painters began working out ideas of their own. They tried to make their figures more lifelike. They learned to paint distant objects smaller than nearer objects, so as to give a sense of distance or depth in their pictures. Examples of early Greek art may be seen in the decorations on vases which have survived to this day.

This new art stressing naturalness and beauty reached its height in Athens under the leadership of Pericles (Pĕr′ĭ klēz) in the fifth century B. C. Everyone became interested in

447

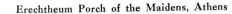

↓ Erechtheum Porch of the Maidens, Athens

By Ewing Galloway, N. Y.

Bronze Statuette: Horse
The Met. Mus. Art

↑ Model of Parthenon, Athens
Courtesy of The Metropolitan Museum of Art

↓ Venus de Milo
By Ewing Galloway, N. Y.

art. Workmen took pride in making fine and lovely things. Greek art is famous for its beauty, good taste, self-restraint, and proportion. It is important for its emphasis on perfection and its great influence on the later development of art.

The original bronze statue of the Discus Thrower has never been found, but there are several Roman copies made of marble. It was sculptured to show the muscles of the body rather than how to throw the discus. Phidias (Fǐd'ǐ ǎs) was the greatest sculptor in the Age of Pericles. Later Greek sculptors created the most perfect and beautiful figures ever found, including the Venus de Milo (Mē'lō).

The most famous buildings of this age were located in Athens on the Acropolis (A krŏp'o lǐs), which means the highest part of a city. They were either civic buildings or temples for gods and goddesses. The Erechtheum (Er ěk thē'ŭm), named for King Erechtheus in Greek mythology, has a porch supported by statues of beautiful maidens. It is the best preserved of these buildings. The finest of all the buildings was the Parthenon (Pär'the nŏn), a temple built for the goddess Athena (A thē'na). The outstanding features of these Greek buildings are their columns, sculptured reliefs, and unattached statues. The Greeks put most of their decorations on the outside, while the Egyptians had adorned the inside. The Greeks usually used white marble. They often painted the hair, lips, eyes, and garments on their statues in colors.

448

# Great Works of Roman Art

After the great period of Grecian art, Rome became the ruling city of many countries. Artists from other nations came to this city, and so art in Rome became a mixture of styles. For instance, the Romans borrowed the idea of portrait busts from the Greeks.

The Romans themselves were great builders. They constructed roads, aqueducts, and public baths. The ruins of these structures amaze the engineers of our day. The Colosseum, which means "gigantic", is a huge amphitheater. It is the most famous of their many buildings. In it the Romans combined the style of Greek temples with old Roman arches. The Pantheon (Păn'thē ŏn), which means "all of the gods", is their grandest

449

The Colosseum

↑ Model of Pantheon, Rome

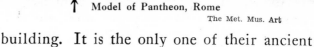

building. It is the only one of their ancient temples still in use. It became a church in early Christian times. It has a domed roof, which is an invention of the Romans.

During the time of Rome's ancient greatness, the inside walls of Roman houses were usually decorated with paintings. Some of these can be seen on the walls of the buildings that have been excavated in Pompeii (Pŏm pā′yē).

From the Mesopotamians (Měs ō pō tā′-mǐ ans) of Asia, the Romans learned the custom of building great columns and arches carved with scenes of the victories of their rulers. Trajan's (Trā′jăn) Column was built in the second century A. D. The Arch of Constantine (Kŏn′stăn tīn) is the best preserved monument of ancient Rome.

450

↓ Arch of Constantine

## Ornate Byzantine Art

Byzantine (Bĭ zăn'tĭn) art grew when Constantine, the first Christian ruler, moved to Byzantium (Istanbul) in 330 A. D. Byzantines loved detail, gilding, mosaics of colored glass and enamel, frescoes, and jewelry. St. Sophia, a church rebuilt with a great dome by the rulers Justinian and Theodora, is the best example of Byzantine architecture. St. Mark's in Venice was rebuilt in this style later.

451

Mosaic: Empress Theodora
The Met. Mus. Art

Saint Mark's Cathedral, Venice
By Ewing Galloway, N. Y.

# The Colorful Art of Persia

The Persians borrowed various ideas of art from other countries, but they insisted on buildings with large, light, airy halls. They decorated their wood and stone buildings with gold, silver, and tiles.

The leaders of the Moslem religion forbade the making of images of living things. So the Moslem Persian artists made lace-like designs known as arabesques for building decorations. They worked out new color combinations for their beautiful hangings and rugs. They made gold and silver jewelry, and cut all kinds of gems.

Later religious leaders allowed the painting of images and pictures that had no connection with their religion. This encouraged artists to illustrate the manuscripts of the classic Persian authors with little paintings. These illustrations are fascinating, fairy-like scenes with doll-like figures. The figures are shown performing acts which clearly represent the action and story illustrated.

The Persians regarded writing as a great and delicate art. The scribes who copied the words became the finest penmen.

452

↓ Persian Animal Rug
Courtesy of The Metropolitan Museum of Art

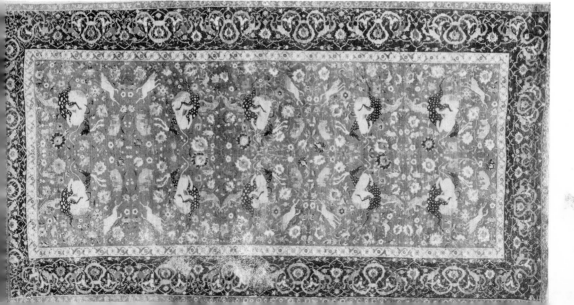